Integrating Your e-Business Enterprise

Andre Yee

Atul Apte

201 West 103rd St., Indianapolis, Indiana, 46290 USA

Integrating Your e-Business Enterprise

Copyright © 2001 by Sams Publishing

International Standard Book Number: 0-672-32056-8

Library of Congress Catalog Card Number: 00-111737

Printed in the United States of America

First Printing: March 2001

03 02 01 00   4 3 2 1

Trademarks

Warning and Disclaimer

ASSOCIATE PUBLISHER
Linda Engelman

ACQUISITIONS EDITOR
Loretta Yates

DEVELOPMENT EDITOR
Clint McCarty

MANAGING EDITOR
Charlotte Clapp

PROJECT EDITOR
Elizabeth Finney

COPY EDITOR
Charles A. Hutchinson

INDEXER
Erika Millen

PROOFREADER
Tony Reitz

TECHNICAL EDITOR
Ankur Laroia

TEAM COORDINATOR
Pamalee Nelson

INTERIOR DESIGNER
Anne Jones

COVER DESIGNER
Anne Jones

PAGE LAYOUT
Lizbeth Patterson

Overview

Table of Contents

About the Authors

Andre Yee is a noted authority on EAI and B2B integration technologies. He has several years of practical experience with middleware and distributed object technologies such as EJB, DCOM, and CORBA. He is a regular conference speaker and has authored several articles on B2B integration, Java, and COM. He was most recently the Vice President, R&D for SAGA Software, a leading provider of e-Business Integration solutions. He currently resides in Northern Virginia.

Atul Apte is the Director, Adapter Development for SAGA Software. He has broad expertise in integrating with various enterprise applications such as SAP, Oracle Applications, and Clarify. He also brings several years of experience in designing and implementing EAI projects for Global 2000 companies. He currently resides in a suburb of Toronto, Canada.

Dedication

To my most excellent wife, Kathy, and my wonderful children, Kirsten, Michael, and Stephen—words of thanks are insufficient. May we live our lives with the ultimate goal—Soli Deo Gloria.

Acknowledgments

First, I would like to thank my coauthor, Atul Apte, for contributing key chapters to this book—in particular, the chapters on interfacing with applications. This book is truly a collaborative effort in every sense.

I also owe many thanks to David Linthicum, Suvajit Gupta, and my friends at SAGA Software for lending support in reviewing, discussing, and challenging my ideas on e-Business Integration. All of you make me better by your participation.

Tell Us What You Think!

As the reader of this book, *you* are our most important critic and commentator. We value your opinion and want to know what we're doing right, what we could do better, what areas you'd like to see us publish in, and any other words of wisdom you're willing to pass our way.

As a Associate Publisher for Sams Publishing, I welcome your comments. You can fax, email, or write me directly to let me know what you did or didn't like about this book—as well as what we can do to make our books stronger.

Please note that I cannot help you with technical problems related to the topic of this book, and that due to the high volume of mail I receive, I might not be able to reply to every message.

When you write, please be sure to include this book's title and author as well as your name and phone or fax number. I will carefully review your comments and share them with the author and editors who worked on the book.

Fax: 317-581-4770
Email: Linda.Engelman@samspublishing.com
Mail: Linda Engelman
            Associate Publisher
            Sams Publishing
            201 West 103rd Street
            Indianapolis, IN 46290 USA

Introduction

A great deal of change has occurred in business over the past few years. The enterprise is no longer simply corporate. It now extends well beyond corporate walls. The Internet is no longer simply a means of communication; it has become a channel for e-Business.

To compete in this new digital economy, companies will have to do more than Web-enable applications, personalize their Web sites, or even modify their business models. In what might initially seem to be an overstatement, I believe that to be truly successful in e-Business, these companies will need to integrate. Classically, integration means connecting newer enterprise information systems with older, legacy data. This process encompasses cohesive integration of both data and business logic. It also means collaboration with partners, suppliers, and customers in an intelligent value chain of products and services. Companies need to be able to link and manage business processes together.

In the end, being able to sell over the Web is not enough; you also need to be able to automatically process orders and fulfill customer needs. That's where *enterprise application integration* (EAI) comes in. EAI allows internal systems to be integrated so that they can provide the automated support needed to fulfill e-Business transactions. In fact, EAI is not simply an enabling function for e-Business; it truly *is* e-Business. It is also insufficient to be able to sell via the Internet but not engage your partners and suppliers in the same fashion. This industrywide epiphany is what accounts for *business-to-business integration* (B2Bi) transactions. As B2Bi grows, it is giving rise to a new emphasis beyond simply point-to-point trading. It is extending to *e-Collaboration*, the need to manage complex business processes and rich relationships between business entities. Whether discussing EAI or B2Bi, you are addressing the need for integration that begins within the enterprise but spans well beyond the enterprise walls to reach partners, suppliers, and customers. This is what is known as *e-Business Integration*.

Who Should Read This Book?

This book is written to be useful to CTOs, CIOs, senior IT managers, project managers, and architects. Each constituent may get something different from the book, but my hope is that all will benefit in some way. Part of what makes e-Business Integration hard to grasp in practice is not only the technology but also fundamental concepts that pave the way to implementation. I believe this book is unique because it blends the concepts together with the technology and practice of e-Business Integration. In this book, you will find help in all three areas.

How This Book Is Organized

How you plan to use this book may depend on your role and what you are trying to accomplish. This book is written to be read cover to cover, and you can certainly choose to do that. You may also find some chapters more useful than others depending on your situation.

Chapters 1 to 3 serve as a broad introduction to e-Business purpose and concepts. Senior executives (CEOs, CIOs, CTOs, and vice presidents) will find these chapters particularly useful as Chapter 1 covers the basic premise of e-Business Integration. Chapters 2 and 3 delve into fundamental technical integration concepts such as the introduction of e-Business Integration architecture (Chapter 2), followed by a discussion of integration patterns (Chapter 3).

Chapters 4 to 9 cover general integration technology elements. This section is critical reading for any IT architect involved in an e-Business Integration project. Discussions of technologies such as integration brokers, application servers, and XML will lend to your integration expertise.

Chapters 10 through 14 discuss the specific integration mechanisms in place to allow integration with primary package applications such as SAP, Siebel, and Peoplesoft, as well as with older technologies such as CICS and 3270 mainframe access. These chapters will provide information pertaining specifically to interfaces to these and other applications. If you don't have an understanding of these interfaces, integration is almost impossible. The heavy lifting occurs when you're navigating the application interfaces in an integration project.

Finally, you have to make your project work. The last two chapters of this book address the issue of methodology and practices that will lead to real success. These chapters provide a series of tips and techniques that will help you during your integration project. Although it is not meant in any way to supplant a book on methodology, this book will cover specific tips regarding integration projects that can prove invaluable.

e-Business Integration Concepts

IN THIS PART

Introduction to e-Business Integration

CHAPTER

1

"There is no reason for any individual to have a computer in his home."
—Kenneth H. Olson, President of DEC,
Convention of the World Future Society, 1977

IN THIS CHAPTER

More than just a technology initiative, conducting e-Business Integration (eBI) is a strategic imperative for most corporations today. eBI encompasses many key operating facets of an organization. eBI initiatives might be "inwardly focused," such as integrating your back office systems, or "outwardly focused," such as linking your corporate processes with those of your partners. Regardless of the particular eBI focus, if you are involved in making integration happen in any fashion, I believe this book will help you. Foremost, you will derive an understanding of the relevant integration technology. I also believe that abstract technical knowledge alone is insufficient. My goal is to provide you with information in a practical context—the kind of information you will need to succeed with your integration project. Hence, the final two chapters in this book deal with methodology and practical tips for success. But first, in this chapter you'll start by learning about the *business* in e-Business Integration. In other words, what is e-Business Integration and why is it important?

What Exactly Is e-Business Integration?

Before now, you may never have heard the term *e-Business Integration*. In reality, e-Business Integration is a new definition for an old problem: the need for applications to exchange business-critical information in real-time.

Almost since the time applications were developed to automate business functions, users have had an integration problem that never seems to go away. In fact, you could say that things have only become worse over time. Whereas once integration problems were confined to the realm of the corporate enterprise, the emergence of e-Business over the past three years has only served to intensify the need for integration. Only now, as Figure 1.1 shows, integration extends beyond the corporate walls to encompass the integration of business-to-consumer (B2C) and business-to-business (B2B) transactions as well.

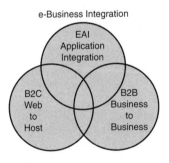

FIGURE 1.1
eBI: EAI, B2C integration, and B2B integration.

eBI is essentially about the end-to-end integration of your business. This includes intra-enterprise integration (that is, the integration of corporate applications within the enterprise) as well as inter-enterprise integration (that is, the integration of data and processes with other corporate enterprises). Intra-enterprise integration has typically been known as *enterprise application integration* (EAI). EAI is primarily about integrating custom and package applications to drive operational efficiency within the corporation. More recently, the significance of EAI has been broadened to encompass the integration of Web-based transactions with corporate applications. That activity, though linked to the Internet, is still primarily an intra-enterprise integration initiative.

In one sense, eBI is simply the natural extension of EAI. Inter-enterprise integration reaches beyond the enterprise to link information from two or more corporate entities. The inter-enterprise model advances the idea of an integrated e-Market composed of discrete transactions from various corporate entities.

e-Business Integration Imperative

When you think about the recent emergence of eBI, you might find yourself asking "Why?" After all, software applications have been around for decades. Why has the need to exchange information between applications become overwhelmingly compelling only recently? I'd like to identify three primary drivers fueling this imperative to integrate.

Mergers and Acquisitions

Some people have described the 1990s as the decade of the global merger, and there are no signs of slowing down. Increased mergers & acquisitions (M&A) activity results in a need to integrate the business processes of corporations worldwide. In every instance, application integration becomes an obvious by-product of the M&A deal.

Integrating shared organizational processes ultimately means integrating the corporate applications that embody those processes. Often the success of an acquisition can rest on how quickly and effectively applications between companies can be integrated.

Rapid Adoption of Package Applications

At times it seems as though no one ever builds applications anymore—not with the preponderance of package applications ranging from customer relationship management (CRM) products to enterprise resource planning (ERP) systems.

In the late 1990s, corporations began making the transition from implementing custom applications to packaged applications. Application vendors such as SAP and Peoplesoft thrived by providing a standard application framework for back office processes such as accounting, billing, and order processing. Highly customizable, these systems could be tailored to the way a particular corporation works.

You might derive from this trend that the need for integration products would potentially diminish. Instead, the deployment of package applications actually reinforces the need for integration. The reason is simply the enduring resilience of legacy applications. It's been commonly noted that the definition of a legacy application is simply an application that works. Despite the rapid adoption of package applications, there remains a base of legacy systems that will likely never be replaced. These legacy applications may perform specialized niche functions inherent to an organization or may simply be cost prohibitive to replace. An industry study noted that 70% of all existing applications in an enterprise are considered "legacy." Integrating corporate business data will necessitate moving information from "legacy" systems to newer package applications and vice versa. Legacy systems still matter and integration architectures must include these systems.

The Emergence of the Internet as a Business Channel

The emergence of the Internet as a business channel has profoundly affected application integration. e-Business has provided a relatively inexpensive channel between individual customers and corporations that supply products and services. The two real technical elements to successful e-business are *interface* and *integration*.

Most of the emphasis in making e-Business work has been on the interface component. In fact, the focus has almost exclusively been on enabling commerce between businesses and consumers. What has largely been ignored until recently is the need for integration in a successful e-Business enterprise. In fact, an AMR Research study revealed that of the 600 leading B2B exchanges, only 10 had application integration built in. eBI means that businesses will not simply capture orders over the Internet but fulfill those orders effectively. Integration is becoming not simply an extension of e-Business but actually a necessary element for success. A leading AMR analyst asserted that exchanges without enterprise integration will eventually end up "dead on the vine."

All this points to the imperative of integration in building a sustainable and scalable e-Business infrastructure. Integration is no longer optional.

The Integration Challenge: How Did We Get Here?

In the early 1990s, most IT organizations were focused on application reengineering, not integration. The centralized corporate application infrastructure (read *mainframe*) was deemed monolithic. The technology cognoscenti at the time endorsed application reengineering as a means to improve efficiency and increase the return on investment (ROI). With the advent of client/server, existing mainframe systems were thought to have a very limited life span. Popular opinion held that newer client/server applications running on inexpensive UNIX boxes would subsume the older mainframe systems.

Yet, as with many bold predictions, the hype fell short of reality. Client/server didn't exactly deliver on the ROI, and the mainframe systems that were supposedly phased-out actually had a far longer life than expected. As it turned out, those systems ran the business and did so far more reliably than the two-tiered client/server architectures of the day. Furthermore, many well-intentioned reengineering projects in the early 1990s often underestimated technical complexity and resulted in significant cost overruns. Even today, most existing mainframe-based systems are not about to be replaced any time soon. They are simply too critical to business function and host decades' worth of corporate data.

Heterogeneous Platforms

The result is a new heterogeneous enterprise that clearly includes a role for the mainframe. However, in this new enterprise, the mainframe is no longer the central focus but simply another operating platform, coexisting with Windows, variants of UNIX such as Solaris, and minicomputer operating systems such as VAX/VMS. To tie applications that span multiple platforms, the integration product must be able to effectively run on each platform. This diverse nature of the corporate enterprise platform lends to the challenge of integration, but it encompasses more than simply the operating system.

Heterogeneous Communications Protocols

Heterogeneity also refers to the various communication channels used to transmit data between systems. Historically, the most common means for data transfer is the *File Transfer Protocol* (FTP). This protocol is limited but thrives because of its simplicity. I will discuss FTP in a little more detail when exploring current technology approaches used for integration in a later chapter.

Another popular protocol employed for distributed computing is the *Transmission Control Protocol/Internet Protocol* (TCP/IP). This protocol is a combination of the *Internet Protocol* (IP), which enables distributed node-to-node data transmission, and *Transmission Control Protocol* (TCP), which provides corrective error management of transmission. Today, most Internet data transfer is conducted via the *Hypertext Transfer Protocol (*HTTP*)*. It is a simple request reply mechanism actually built on top of IP.

Integrating the e-Business enterprise means traversing the differences in these and other communication protocols as well as operating systems.

Corporate "Islands of Automation"

The move away from a centralized host to distributed client/server environment paved the way for a more diverse set of application products, serving the needs of a given department or division. The idea of autonomy superseded the need for corporate consistency and application unity. The introduction of *commercial off the shelf* (COTS) applications only led to a proliferation of independent, automated stovepipes. These departmental-level stovepipes may be highly efficient but in effect caused the notion of the enterprise resembling "islands of automation" to emerge. Figure 1.2 depicts the stovepipe effect of independent, automated departments disconnected from each other.

FIGURE 1.2

The stovepipe effect: corporate islands of automation.

The formation of these "islands of automation" consisting of business applications that exist independently moved the focus from application reengineering to application integration. Today, many IT executives believe that integration is the primary technical problem that will confront them in the coming years.

Data Syntax

What makes it difficult to integrate the enterprise is that each application manages and externalizes data in distinct formats that are often proprietary in nature. SAP modules will likely externalize data as *interface documents* (IDOCs). These large, text-based documents encapsulate critical business data in a repeating data file format. On the other hand, most databases store information in a relational form and allow for data to be retrieved via a Structured Query Language (SQL) interface. Newer Web-based applications may both store and externalize data as XML documents. Rather than supplant existing data formats as a universal format, XML adds to the data syntax problem. In a typical corporate enterprise, integration must involve the translating syntax differences between the diverse application data that exist. This means translating native data formats between applications within the enterprise as well as transforming XML-based documents between business entities.

Application Semantics

The fundamental effect of a distributed enterprise is an increased number and diversity of applications that comprise the corporate application framework. This corporate application framework may be composed of decades-old legacy applications, Web-based sales automation, and an Electronic Data Interchange (EDI) gateway. When you attempt to integrate these different systems, it becomes apparent that data reformatting and translation are insufficient. It is necessary to exchange information, not simply data. Moving *information* between applications involves more than simply translating data formats. Information integration involves transmitting both the *context* as well as the *contents* of the data packet. This process is often known as *translating application semantics*. The representation of a business object in a simple billing application is typically different from the way it might be represented in a corporate enterprise application. The translation of that information necessitates the application of transformation rules to ensure that the data is moved from one context to another without loss of semantic value in the common data elements.

Middleware Revolution

The mid-1990s heralded the emergence of *middleware* as a unique technology layer that enabled the access and transport of data between different application entities. The evolution of middleware resulted in a segmentation of four distinct categories:

- Data access middleware
- Object middleware
- Transaction processing middleware
- Message queuing middleware

Although these technologies attempted to address the enterprise integration problem, the distinct limitations of each technology have left the industry seeking a better solution.

The integration problem as I've described it in this section deals with EAI, or enterprise application integration. However, the Internet has changed the notion of the enterprise, extending it beyond corporate boundaries.

Internet: Extending the Enterprise

Integration has become a lot more complex in the past three years. During that time, the Internet evolved from a communication facility into a legitimate business channel. The Internet is the catalyst transforming and extending EAI into e-Business Integration. It has led to the model being extended in two primary ways: Web-to-enterprise integration and B2B integration.

Web-to-Enterprise

Web-to-enterprise integration is the natural extension of what is known as *web-to-host*. Web-to-host has typically been applied to technologies that have been used to Web-enable legacy systems. As shown in Figure 1.3, web-to-enterprise involves integrating the Web interface with the rest of the enterprise applications.

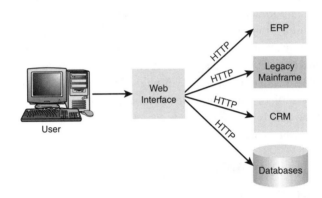

FIGURE 1.3
Web-to-enterprise integration.

In this model, the focus is not merely Web-based data access as in a Web-to-host environment but on integrating Web interfaces as part of the overall integration flow.

B2B Integration (B2Bi)

According to the industry analyst group, Forrester, B2B commerce is estimated to balloon to $6.3 trillion by 2004. Although trading between companies has existed for many years in the form of Electronic Data Interchange (EDI) trading hubs, B2B brings a new twist. Unlike EDI, B2B involves the use of a public network, the Internet. This open network means easy accessibility for any business entity that wants to participate. Second, B2B business transactions are dynamic, unlike the static processes within the EDI model. B2B integration is simply the enabler for business transactions between corporate entities. Although B2Bi is fundamentally just integration, and many corollaries can be derived from EAI, a couple of aspects are unique to the trade space.

Although EAI is all about integrating applications, B2Bi is about integrating corporate entities. EAI products have been designed to tie together enterprise applications, not necessarily corporate trading partners. Integrating enterprise applications requires conversion of application native data, whereas integrating B2B involves translating between XML-based documents. (Chapter 2 explores this topic in more detail.) B2Bi and EAI will require fundamentally different technologies. EAI demands the conversion and transformation of native data as primary value. B2Bi, however, does not primarily deal with complex native data formats but rather XML-based documents externalized out of the enterprise. This means that integration is not quite as complex and generally involves reformatting between text-based documents. The difference is also evident in that EAI is primarily concerned with the flow of data exchange, but B2Bi emphasizes the process of data exchange between participants. This means a focus in Business Process Integration (BPI) is essential, not optional for B2B.

How to Succeed with eBI

One point most experts will agree on is that eBI is difficult to solve because integration projects in general require very diverse skills. Both technical as well as business analysis skills are needed. On the technical side, practitioners must be knowledgeable in native application interfaces. Often this can be extremely time and resource intensive. Among other skills, technical staff must be adept at data modeling as well. Simply put, putting the project team together is a challenge. Another common barrier to success is simply the adoption or use of tools that are inadequate for the tasks at hand. Many available tools are limited in the capability to solve the end-to-end eBI problem, encompassing EAI as well as B2Bi. Finally, integration projects are inherently and typically complex. Practical advice on how to approach these kinds of projects is hard to come by, much less a formal methodology.

I'd like to propose that there is a way to enhance the opportunity for a successful eBI initiative. It includes the following:

- Understanding e-Business Integration concepts
- Understanding e-Business Integration technologies
- Understanding e-Business Integration practices

Summary

This book is organized to take you through a discussion of e-Business concepts, technologies, and practices in a way I hope you will find coherent and effective. This first chapter has provided some of the groundwork upon which subsequent chapters will build.

In Chapter 2, "e-Business Concepts and Architecture," you will begin to explore the e-Business Integration concepts. This will eventually lead to a discussion of a new technical architecture. The e-Business Integration architecture will provide a coherent view and taxonomy of integration technologies.

e-Business Concepts and Architecture

"No architecture can be truly noble which is not imperfect."
—John Ruskin

IN THIS CHAPTER

e-Business Integration encompasses far more than simply "connecting the dots" between various applications. It entails moving information intelligently, not simply between applications but other logical entities that may represent corporate organizations or communities. This calls for a new integration architecture that can extend beyond data or application integration today. The tri-pronged focus of this chapter is as follows:

1. To shed light on how integration is accomplished today and some of the limitations of existing approaches

2. To introduce the e-Business Integration Architecture

3. To explain common integration concepts

This chapter acts as a launching pad to discuss, in future chapters, a number of key technologies that are pertinent to the architecture. The discussion here begins with some of the traditional approaches to integration and their limitations.

Existing Approaches and Their Limitations

Many integration approaches are undoubtedly tried and true. Four technical solutions are commonly applied, each having its own distinct strengths and weaknesses:

- Point-to-Point File Transfer
- Database Gateways
- Object Middleware
- Message Queuing Middleware

Point-to-Point File Transfer Systems

The Point-to-Point File Transfer Protocol (PTP-FTP) may be the most commonly used mechanism for transferring data from one application to another. The essence of how PTP-FTP works is fairly simple. Data is exported from the source application into a flat file. The file is transferred to a target system via FTP, and the file is subsequently imported into a target application. Figure 2.1 depicts how this works. The advantage of PTP-FTP is that implementing it is technically simple. Its evident lack of sophistication is actually part of the appeal of this approach.

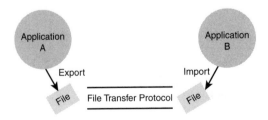

FIGURE 2.1
Point-to-Point File Transfer.

However, the disadvantages of PTP-FTP are also obviously apparent. This approach is predicated on a "hard contract" between both systems. The source application must export a fixed data set in with a specified format. Similarly, the target application expects to receive a fixed data set to import. Often that logic to be able to export and receive the predefined data sets ends up being tightly coupled to the application. This results in a brittle system. Any data-related changes, either in terms of extending the data set or changing the data types, could cause that system to fail if the application is not similarly altered to export and import the new data formats.

Another disadvantage is related to the actual data transfer mechanism. With PTP-FTP, data transfer procedures are conducted in a batch mode and do not accommodate "near–real-time" or "low-latency" scenarios. Facilities for guaranteed data delivery and failed data recovery are virtually nonexistent with this approach. Consequently, this method is generally deemed unreliable for timely delivery of mission-critical data.

Finally, point-to-point integrated systems are generally difficult to manage. Proliferation of numerous point-to-point connections lead to what is commonly known as the "application integration spaghetti"—a set of individual and independent links that are inherently unmanageable.

Database Gateways

Database gateways provide more than simply a data access mechanism to a single database. Database gateways actually provide a means to unlock data from multiple applications. They typically allow for integration of data from multiple disparate databases via a SQL-oriented query facility. As depicted in Figure 2.2, the idea is that through the use of a database gateway, you are able to integrate data from Oracle running on UNIX, MS-SQL Server on Windows NT, and DB2 on a mainframe. This is clearly far more than simply data access through ODBC or JDBC drivers. In effect, it creates a "virtual database" where multiple disparate databases can be accessed as easily as accessing a solitary database. The database gateway maps the incoming request to a join of multiple discrete requests. Each returned data set is joined together to provide a consolidated reply. Database gateways are often used to integrate data from different back-end data resources with a client-side application. Examples of database gateways include EDA/SQL from Information Builders and IBM's Distributed Relational Data Access (DRDA).

Database gateways are effective in brokering client requests over multiple data resources, but used for the purposes of e-Business Integration, they carry specific limitations. Database gateways are often too inefficient for server-side application integration because they can adapt to applications only in a purely request-reply mode. Obtaining application data is predicated on issuing a SQL query and extracting data records. The inability to receive application-initiated events results in having to poll the application databases periodically. Having to do so can be exceedingly inefficient when you're dealing with multiple applications.

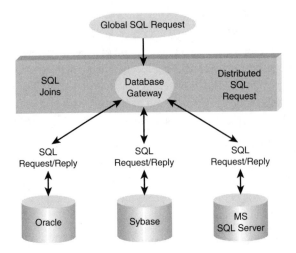

FIGURE 2.2

Database gateway integration.

Another problem with a database-centric approach to integration is that the context of how that data relates to business rules (that is, the application logic) is bypassed. This business logic then must be represented separately outside the context of the application. Sometimes this is done through programmable SQL queries, but it leads to duplicity in logic that must be maintained.

Object Middleware

Object middleware products such as those based on Common Object Request Broker Architecture (CORBA) or Microsoft's own Component Object Model (COM+) provide a component model, distributed services, and supporting tools. Both CORBA and COM+ allow developers to create components that encapsulate application logic. These components communicate and interoperate via an object bus at runtime. Distributed services such as those for security, naming, transaction, and event management are provided in support of these components. Among the leading CORBA products are Orbix (IONA) and VisiBroker (Inprise).

As an integration technology, object middleware provides a reliable synchronous channel for communication between source and target applications. However, because object middleware typically operates through a synchronous channel, it requires that both applications are available and ready to participate in the integration. Message auditing, important for e-Business Integration scenarios, is typically not a built-in facility within the object middleware architecture. It must be implemented externally and can be fairly intrusive. Tracking and rationalizing data from multiple sources as encountered in complex integration flows will require that significant code be written. The role of component integration architectures is discussed later in this chapter.

Message Queuing Middleware

Message Queuing Middleware (MQM) or Message Oriented Middleware (MOM) is predicated on asynchronous messaging. Asynchronous messaging products have been around since the 1970s and are proven reliable mechanisms for data communication. Asynchronous messaging provides three advantages when used for application integration:

• Ability to handle intermittent application availability

• Ability to support complex message routing

• Ability to support advanced services

Handling Intermittent Availability

Asynchronous messaging allows for intermittent availability, which means that a receiver of the data doesn't have to be available for the producer of the data to transmit data. Synchronous mechanisms, on the other hand, are predicated on establishing an open channel for communication. Although they can perform better at a point-to-point level, they require that both the sender and receiver be available and ready in order to communicate. MQM products operate on what some have called a "fire and forget" model. It is a loosely coupled system in which the MQM software intermediates between the two applications, as shown in Figure 2.3.

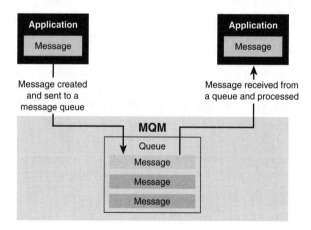

FIGURE 2.3
Message Queuing Middleware.

Whether the receiver is not available doesn't really matter to the sender because the MQM product essentially acts as the intermediary for message transmission.

Support for Complex Routing of Messages

MQM products can handle complex routing of messages that are inherent in enterprise application integration (EAI). Application integration calls for the ability to receive one or more input messages and, after completion of processing, the ability to send one or more resulting output messages.

Support for Advanced Services

MQM products on the market include the MQ Series from IBM, Microsoft's MSMQ, and Level 8's FalconMQ. These products can provide advanced services such as security facilities, guaranteed delivery, and message persistence. Each of these services is necessary to provide e-Business enterprise scale integration. Additionally, most MQM products provide sophisticated trace and audit messages, not typically available in synchronous communication mechanisms.

Until recently, one drawback to MQM was the lack of a consistent, standard messaging model. Messaging functionality represented in MQM products varied considerably. However, it appears that the emergence of the Java Messaging Service (JMS) specification is beginning to receive broad industry support as most vendors provide conformance to that standard. Another limitation of MQM in application integration is that many of the necessary elements of integrating applications such as the data transformation, formatting, and routing of data based on business rules are not inherently provided. This means that the developer is left to re-create them by building a set of services in the form of an intermediate application. Recently, a new specialized category of messaging-based products known as *integration brokers* has emerged to address this need in a seamless fashion. Many of these products work in conjunction with the MQM product.

New Technology Framework for e-Business Integration

As you learned previously, these technologies have distinct advantages as well as disadvantages. When applied appropriately, they can be extremely effective.

However, the imperative to integrate both within the enterprise (EAI) as well as beyond the enterprise boundaries (B2Bi) creates new requirements and necessitates a new technology framework. This framework, shown in Figure 2.4, must address both intra-enterprise integration as well as inter-enterprise integration, linking relevant internal corporate information together with those of partners and suppliers.

Why a new framework? Isn't integration the same whether applied internally or externally? It may appear so in concept, but as you'll learn later, there are subtle differences between EAI and B2B integration (B2Bi).

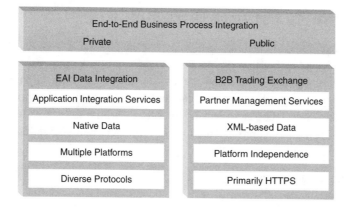

FIGURE 2.4

e-Business technology framework.

These differences translate into different functional and architectural emphasis in technologies. As an example, for EAI, translating application-native data types is extremely important. On the other hand, B2Bi data exchanges tend to be XML based, and translation occurs between text-based documents. In this case, although emerging technologies such as eXtensible Style Language for Transformations (XSLT) may be appropriate for B2Bi, it will probably not suffice for EAI.

Also, assumptions made in addressing the EAI problem may not be valid for the B2Bi space. In EAI, multiplatform support is a distinct advantage. The need to integrate with applications that run on various operating platforms necessitates that elements of the integration solution are also enabled to run those platforms as well. In B2Bi, the platform issue might be deemed irrelevant when transacting with external business entities because no assumptions can be made about your partner's operating platform. In the B2Bi scenario, each participant may deploy a different integration product, and it is sub-optimal to require that a component of your integration solution be installed at your partner's site. Consistent data exchange is achieved through a common self-describing document format like XML and a defined process for business engagement.

In essence, the incorporation of B2Bi to engage integration with external business entities has altered the scope and nature of integration. With B2Bi, the integrated entities are not applications but business organizations, hence requiring a different set of services such as partner profile management, trading notification, and collaboration services. Data exchange format is normalized, whereas native data translation is de-emphasized. Relationships and interactions are more complex and rich, requiring the process of interaction to be actively managed. It makes Business Process Integration (BPI) both necessary and compelling. Therefore, encompassing both the EAI and B2Bi worlds is the modeling, monitoring, and management of business processes.

The e-Business Integration Architecture

The e-Business Integration Architecture is a conceptual integration service architecture. It defines a layered view of technology and tools needed for e-Business Integration. It is a useful way of representing e-Business Integration because it provides an "integration worldview"— that is, the taxonomy framework to interpret and understand integration as applied to e-Business. It would include necessary elements for inter-enterprise as well as intra-enterprise integration. The e-Business Integration Architecture shown in Figure 2.5 delineates four layers of integration tools and services:

- Transport integration layer
- Data integration layer
- Interface integration layer
- Process integration layer

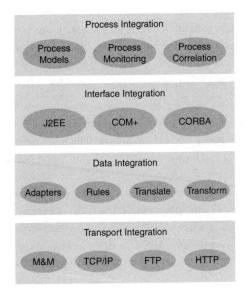

FIGURE 2.5

e-Business Integration Architecture.

Each layer addresses a different and increasingly complex level of integration as you move up the stack. Each layer operates not in exclusion but rather cohesively with the other layers. As you'll discover in the next chapter, integration problems can be divided into many classes. In solving a particular type of integration problem, you may employ technologies spanning all four or only one of these layers. In any event, this architecture stack will help you understand the taxonomy of integration technologies and how they work together. Starting with the Transport integration layer, the following sections examine each layer in terms of function and technology.

Transport Integration Layer

The Transport integration layer provides communication channels for linking and moving data between two or more points of integration. This is the most basic level of integration, moving data packages from point A to point B. Integration may take place at the protocol level where two systems exchange data through establishing a common protocol for communication or through the use of more sophisticated concepts such as message queues. Technologies that fall into this category cover a broad range from fundamental protocols such as Internet Protocol (IP) to messaging products such as MQ Series. In either case, the underlying premise is embodied in the idea of connecting systems by moving data through a transport layer.

TCP/IP is a commonly used protocol in the movement of data within and beyond the enterprise walls. Although TCP/IP may appear to be a singular protocol, it is actually composed of layers. Internet Protocol (IP) allows for movement of data from node to node in a global network. Each node is assigned an IP address, and each transmitted data packet contains a destination address known as the IP number. Transmission Control Protocol (TCP) is responsible for verifying correct data delivery from client to server. TCP provides error detection and data retransmission in the event that data is not delivered correctly or completely. You will often hear the use of the term *sockets* in conjunction with TCP/IP. Sockets such as WinSock are a set of functions that allow the utilization of TCP/IP.

The most common transport of B2B data over the Internet still occurs through the use of the Hypertext Transfer Protocol (HTTP). HTTP is basically a protocol for request/reply communication and typically operates over TCP/IP connections. The protocol of interaction works by an HTTP client initiating a request to be fulfilled by a server. This process may involve a single direct connection between the client and server. At times, an intermediary may be involved between the client and server. Three types of intermediaries may be in play: proxies, gateways, or tunnels. A proxy forwards the request to the server identified in the URI after receiving and reformatting the message. A gateway receives the message and translates it on behalf of the server. A tunnel moves messages between firewalls without changing the contents of the messages in any way. HTTP is amazingly simple to use, which lends to it remaining the *de facto* transport standard for data interchange over the Internet.

In discussing transport, you will discover references to *synchronous* and *asynchronous* as fundamental paradigms for data transfer. Synchronous communication requires a channel to be established and maintained between sender and receiver for communication to occur. In this mode, the paradigm of data transfer is typically request-reply in nature. A client sends a request and is typically blocked until the request is fulfilled. Synchronous communication is often applied when real-time communication is required, but it necessitates that both sender and receiver are up and available. Examples include distributed computing technologies such as the Distributed Computing Environment Remote Procedure Call (DCE-RPC) or Java Remote Method Invocation (RMI). Technically speaking, both these technologies also belong in the Interface integration layer. However, RPC and RMI still represent the most commonly used mechanisms for synchronous communication.

The asynchronous communication paradigm allows the sender to be loosely coupled from the receiver. A client may send messages continuously without being blocked, while the receiver consumes the messages on the other end. This capability is particularly advantageous when the sender and receiver may be only intermittently connected such as with mobile applications. The most common example today of the asynchronous messaging paradigm applied would include the use of message queuing products such as MQ Series and MSMQ. Both these products dominate the message queuing market. As you learned previously, message queuing products function as an intermediary between two or more systems. Message queuing products are particularly adept at managing multiple sender and receiver entities at once. Unlike synchronous mechanisms that establish point-to-point connections, the message queuing server conducts session management and audits data flow.

Data Integration Layer

The Data integration layer goes beyond simply transporting data packets between two points. Integrating applications effectively requires far more than the transmission and transformation of data. Regardless of the technical solution chosen, to successfully integrate two applications, you have to be able to address application access, application syntax, and application semantics.

Application access refers to the ability to extract data from and insert data into the application data store. This also applies to the ability to extract application meta data whenever available. The ability to extract application meta data may be variable to a great extent, depending on both the nature of the application and the method employed for data access. For instance, some enterprise resource planning (ERP) applications provide meta data accessible through a defined API. On the other hand, accessing a mainframe legacy system through screen scrapping provides no opportunity to extract meta data.

Application data must be translated from the syntax of the source application to that of the destination application(s). In today's heterogeneous environment, this may mean translating between XML-based data from your Web application into a proprietary ADABAS data store on the OS/390.

Application semantics is a necessary condition for complex application integration. It simply means that when raw data is transformed and transmitted from one application to another, the context of the data must be interpreted as well. For example, if you integrate a Web order entry system with a corporate customer management database, you may discover that the data definition of a customer in the Web-based system is significantly more simplistic than in the corporate customer database. The customer object for the Web-based application may be defined by a record with a six-character alphanumeric identifier and 10 corresponding customer-related fields. On the other hand, the corporate database definition of customer-related data may span several tables linked together by three indexed keys, each with a prefix. Transforming from one definition of customer to another requires intelligent mapping of the customer object from one context to another.

A core set of services for data-level integration is required to deliver on all three points related to integrating application. These core elements of application integration address the complexities of application access, syntax, and semantics. They include the following:

- Application Adapters
- Translation Framework
- Transformation Service
- Data Integration Rules

Application Adapters
Application adapters enable you to access the application. Adapters may achieve access through various means, including going directly to the database, utilizing application APIs, or employing other unconventional means such as screen scraping. Several chapters later in this book are devoted to discussing adapters in general and also the mechanisms used to access some of the most popular applications.

Translation Framework
The translation framework is responsible for the conversion and translation of data syntax. The translation activity may involve native data types or purely text-based documents as are increasingly popular today in the B2B space.

Transformation Service
The transformation service is also known at times as a *formatter*. The transformation service reformats *n* input messages into *m* output messages. Strictly speaking, transformation is broader than simply reformatting messages. It includes operational computation as well. Besides the task of reformatting, it may also involve taking an element within a message and performing an operation on it before writing it out into a newly formatted message.

Data Integration Rules
Data integration rules allow for the semantics of the application data to be properly interpreted. As a rule (sorry—I couldn't resist), they should not be confused with business rules that may be more verbose or rules characteristic of inference engines. Data integration rules tend to be

simple and are typically conditional and governed by sequentially processed Boolean logic.
Data integration rules supply conditions for data conversion and parameters for mapping.

Integration Brokers

Assuming you're convinced that all these services are necessary for data-level integration, how
would you begin to piece these elements together? You could seek to acquire a transformation
engine, for example, and write your own adapters. The good news is that you don't have to.
Over the past few years, a class of technology products has emerged to provide that capability
and more. These products are known as *message brokers* or *integration brokers*. Integration brokers bring together these fundamental elements of data-level integration within a single cohesive
unit, generally driven through both a programmatic as well as a graphical design interface.
Integration brokers will be discussed in greater detail in Chapter 4, "Integration Brokers."

Interface Integration Layer

Enterprise applications consist of presentation, business logic and data. Whereas the Data integration layer addresses only the sharing of application data, the Interface integration layer, also
known as Method integration, allows for the sharing of business logic between applications.
Many newer applications are constructed with a distributed component architecture, so this
layer could legitimately be referred to as the Component integration layer as well. Because
components externalize interfaces as a point of access, the integration of components is
described as *interface integration*. Regardless of the name used, the idea revolves around the
integration of business logic through the invocation of function calls.

Applications, whether expressed in modules or components, may contain important business
logic. Often sharing this logic between applications is more efficient than "reinventing the
wheel." Sharing promotes reusability of business logic throughout the corporation and ensures
consistency. As an example, ACME Manufacturing wants to upgrade its Customer
Management System to conduct periodic credit risk analysis on its customers. However, that
same functionality is already part of the Sales Automation System that allows for the same risk
analysis to be conducted on a prospective customer. Instead of developing that facility within
the Customer Management System, wouldn't it be beneficial to reuse that logic encapsulated
within the Sales Management System? That is precisely what is accomplished in this layer of
integration. Although it is not commonly thought of in this fashion, the sharing of business
logic through callable interfaces is essentially integration. As shown in Figure 2.6, the Interface
integration layer allows for intermediary application code to be developed to bridge two separate applications together.

Figure 2.6
Interface-level integration.

The practical implication of this type of integration occurring today is through the use of distributed components as a means of encapsulating business logic. CORBA and Microsoft's COM+ are two examples of component technology in action. COM+ defines a component model supported by a rich set of component services such as the transaction management and queued components. It is also supported by a broad set of development tools. Alas, COM+ is available only on the Windows platform, which limits its application for true enterprise use.

CORBA is a distributed object specification that is the resulting work of the Object Management Group (OMG), an industry consortium representing nearly 800 companies. CORBA operates on an object bus that allows each component to make dynamic method invocations. CORBA allows the creation and management of objects that are transactional, secure, and persistent.

More recently, Sun Microsystems has introduced its own component model known as Enterprise Java Beans (EJB). EJB is a server-side component model. It allows the development and deployment of object-oriented distributed applications. The EJB components can be hosted within application servers that provide EJB container support. Like CORBA, these EJB components can be transactional, secure, and persistent. EJB together with other enterprise standards such as Java Database Connectivity (JDBC) and Java Messaging Service (JMS) are part of the Java 2 Enterprise Edition (J2EE) platform.

Process Integration Layer

The Process integration layer enables the integration of business processes. Rather than being primarily focused on integrating physical entities such as data or business components, Business Process Integration (BPI) involves the integration of logical entities represented as business process elements. Instead of being driven by the transport and transformation of data, BPI emerges from linking together activity-driven business processes. The entities linked together are not defined as information but rather in terms of activity or workflow. For instance, in linking together the elements of the Sales Orders Process, BPI does so with entities expressed as "Sales Order Received," "Verify Credit," or "Check Inventory." Figure 2.7 depicts a Sales Order Process beginning with a "Sales Order Received" trigger event that starts the process.

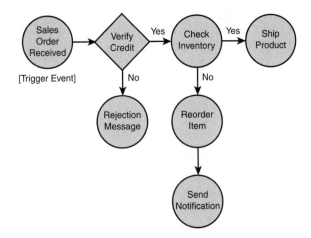

FIGURE 2.7
Sales Order Business Process.

Of course, all logical representation must map to physical elements. "Check Inventory Levels" ultimately means issuing a request to the Inventory Management System and applying a test to the result. BPI is actually composed of different components that perform different aspects of process integration. The three fundamental components of BPI are as follows:

Business Process Modeler—Allows the user to model the integrated enterprise as interlinked business process activities

Business Process Broker—Manages the runtime workflow processes

Business Process Management—Monitors the flow of business processes and the correlation of process events with business metrics

Rather than explore these components now, you'll examine them in more detail when you look at BPI in Chapter 6, "Understanding Business Process Integration."

Summary

In this chapter, I've discussed the limitations of existing integration technologies such as point-to-point FTP, database gateways, object and message queueing middleware. Also in this chapter, you've been introduced to the e-Business integration architecture composed of four primary integration layers—transport, data, interface, and process integration. Chapter 3, "e-Business Integration Patterns," will introduce the concept of integration patterns. It will emphasize the importance of patterns and define the idea of an integration pattern. You will also examine seven distinct patterns that represent primary applied e-Business Integration categories.

e-Business Integration Patterns

"Consistency is the last refuge of the unimaginative."
—Oscar Wilde

IN THIS CHAPTER

e-Business Integration occurs in as many forms as there are e-Businesses. At first glance, integration problems and the corresponding solutions are seldom identical. Yet, upon closer examination, you discover that integration solutions can actually be classified into common categories. Each of these categories describes both a "type" of integration problem as well as a solution method. These categories are called *integration patterns*. Integration patterns help you understand the different methods available to you for a given type of integration problem. They allow you to take a step back and understand the differences in the various scenarios and appreciate the different approaches to integration. Finally, they allow you to view "integration in the big picture." You can learn to break down what may be a complex integration into conceptual categories and understand which technologies to apply.

What Are Integration Patterns?

A *pattern* is commonly defined as a reliable sample of traits, acts, tendencies, or other observable characteristics. In software development, you may be familiar with the idea of *design patterns* or *process patterns*. Design patterns systematically describe object designs that can be employed for a common set of problems. Similarly, process patterns describe proven methods and processes used in software development. In practice, patterns are simply a logical classification of commonly recurring actions, techniques, designs, or organizations.

What are integration patterns? Integration patterns emerge from classification of standard solutions for integration scenarios. They are not patterns of design or code. Nor are they patterns of operational processes for an integration project. Instead, each integration pattern defines a type of integration problem, a solution technique, as well as parameters applied for e-Business Integration.

I have identified seven common e-Business Integration patterns. They are not meant to be comprehensive, but they cover most of the common integration scenarios implemented today. They encompass both EAI scenarios as well as B2Bi scenarios:

EAI (intra-enterprise) Patterns

- Database Replication
- Single-Step Application Integration
- Multi-Step Application Integration
- Brokering Application

B2Bi (inter-enterprise) Patterns

- Application-to-Application B2Bi
- Data Exchange B2Bi
- B2B Process Integration

The EAI Patterns represent patterns commonly applied within a corporate enterprise, whereas the B2Bi Patterns represent the different methods in conducting integrated B2B transactions. The following sections provide a closer look at each of these patterns and discuss some of the details.

Database Replication

The Database Replication pattern may be the most prevalent pattern of EAI integration today. Database replication involves managing copies of data over two or more databases, resulting in redundant data. Companies engage in database replication for numerous reasons. One reason is that many organizations are becoming more distributed in their operations, requiring multiple copies of the same data over several physical locations. Replication is also a means of data recovery. In many organizations, an active secondary database is maintained for data recovery purposes. In the event that the production database needs to be recovered, the secondary replicated database can be used. This also applies for "high availability" systems. In these situations, a redundant copy of "live" data is maintained to ensure that if the first system is not available, the redundant database system is activated.

The two general categories for database replication are synchronous and asynchronous replication.

Synchronous Replication

Synchronous replication involves maintaining absolute consistency between source and target databases. The primary objective is to ensure real-time data consistency between the databases. This is what is known as *achieving zero latency* between the data resources. In practice, this calls for the use of transaction processing technology in order to ensure absolute data consistency. Figure 3.1 depicts the use of transaction processing monitor in replication.

Transactions must conform to what is commonly known as the *ACID* properties. This means that transaction operations must be Atomic, Consistent, Isolated, and Durable:

Description of the ACID properties

Atomic—A transaction is atomic when the system treats each transaction discretely as a single call that either succeeds or fails.

Consistent—This attribute means that the transaction component or object is changed from one valid state to another.

Isolated—The operation of a transaction is isolated from other transactions.

Durable—Transactions that are committed are permanent even if the system fails.

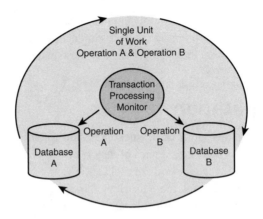

FIGURE 3.1

Synchronous replication with transaction processing.

Using the transactional protocol means that the brokering of data across the databases must be accomplished as a single unit of work. Discrete data changes to Database A are simultaneously made to Database B. If the data changes are successful for Database A but not successful for Database B, the changes for Database A are "rolled back" and both systems are returned to the previously consistent state. As mentioned previously, this kind of transaction processing between both systems is achieved through the use of a transaction processing monitor (TPM) such as CICS (IBM) or Tuxedo (BEA).

Asynchronous Replication

Asynchronous replication has a much looser latency requirement. The time required for all systems to be "in sync" or consistent is an observable measure of time. This doesn't mean that the need to maintain transactional integrity is diminished in any way. It is still necessary to ensure that discrete data elements are moved as a single unit of work. Asynchronous message queuing products such as MQ Series are often used to preserve transactional semantics as part of the replication process. They do so through the use of transactional queues. Transactional queues guarantee that the data delivery process is not completed until the data packet inserted into the queue by the source database is de-queued and committed to the target data resource.

Single-Step Application Integration

The Single-Step Application Integration (SSAI) pattern extends the asynchronous database replication pattern. Instead of focusing on data consistency between two databases, the SSAI pattern integrates data between applications, moving data from one context to another. It does so by translating data syntax of the source message and reformatting data elements into a new target message. It is "single step" because it requires an intermediary broker to map source messages to target messages. Typically, it is an extension of the asynchronous replication technology, in that it utilizes Message Queuing Middleware such as MQ Series. It is just as likely to be implemented with the less sophisticated FTP in a batch mode. In either case, the point is that it does more than simply move data from point A to point B for consistency's sake. Whereas, in the replication pattern both the source and target data models are likely similar, if not identical at times, this is not necessarily the case for the SSAI pattern. The objective here is not data consistency, but application data integration. Figure 3.2 illustrates an example of SSAI where message A is directly transformed to message B.

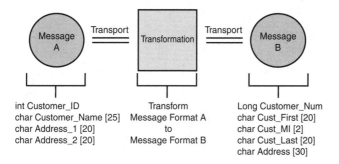

FIGURE 3.2
Single-Step Application Integration.

SSAI brokers perform a single-step transformation involving the translation, reformatting, and application of rules to intelligently map data from one point to another. However, the entire "transaction" is still point-to-point in nature. Although integration of multiple enterprisewide applications can be treated as a series of point-to-point integration instances, doing so has limitations and necessitates a more flexible and complex pattern.

Multi-Step Application Integration

The Multi-Step Application Integration (MSAI) pattern is an extension of the SSAI pattern. MSAI enables the integration of n (source) to m (target) applications. It addresses many-to-many integration, which SSAI cannot, by providing what is known as *sequential logical processing*. In other words, steps in this pattern are processed sequentially, and rules applied are Boolean logical in nature. Like the single-step pattern, MSAI requires an intermediary to broker the transaction of data between applications. It is often built around an asynchronous event-based system and typically is implemented through the use of Message Queuing Middleware as well. The asynchronous event-based approach creates loose coupling. Although each system is physically independent, they are logically dependent. In other words, interdependencies exist between the application events that can be expressed in terms of transformations and data integration rules. Data elements from one application can drive the retrieval or processing of messages in another application.

The simplest multi-step example in Figure 3.3 involves three applications in which a message from application A is combined with a message from application B that is reformatted for a target application C. It is common for a data element from application A to act as a key to drive the request for information from application B.

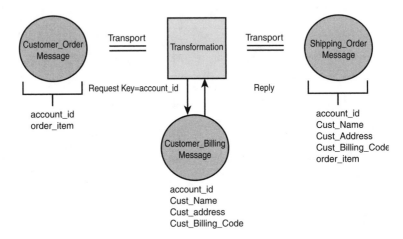

FIGURE 3.3

Multi-Step Application Integration.

In Figure 3.3, the `account_id` data element from the `Customer_Order` message is used as the key for a request for a `Customer_Billing` message from the application. Data elements from both messages are combined and transformed according to the applicable data conversion rules to deliver a `Shipping_Order` message to the Shipping & Distribution System. Even in a trivial example like this, you can see how the `Customer_Billing` message has logical dependency on the `Customer_Order` message. The final `Shipping_Order` message depends on elements of both the `Customer_Order` and `Customer_Billing` messages.

You can, of course, see many more complex variations of the multi-step processing in the example. For instance, instead of just getting the customer billing information, what if the `Customer_Order` message provided the product codes to allow a check of the inventory system? Each product on the `Customer_Order` message would be checked for product availability. For *n* number of order items, this would generate *n* number of look-ups to the inventory system. Depending on the outcome, multiple output messages could be generated, such as a customer notification email or an entry to the vendors database to generate a reorder of inventory. In this more complex example, multiple outputs can occur. The MSAI pattern is an extensive and flexible pattern allowing for complex application integration to occur.

Brokering Application

As you learned in Chapter 2, "e-Business Concepts and Architecture," at times integrating two applications is not principally a matter of integrating data, but integrating business logic. The Brokering Application pattern addresses the use of intermediary application logic to link together two or more applications. In plain terms, it means that custom application code is written containing logic to broker interactions between the disparate applications. This custom brokering application sits in the middle as an intermediary for processing requests from different applications, as shown in Figure 3.4.

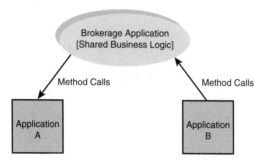

FIGURE 3.4
Brokering Application.

The use of this solution pattern is particularly applicable in the scenarios presented in the following sections.

Applications Need to Reuse Logic

The Brokering Application pattern may often be used effectively when two or more applications need to share or reuse common business logic. For instance, if application A contains business logic for a specific calculation and other applications can use such calculation logic, you can write intermediary custom code to access the logic from application A. In this case, the intermediary brokering application acts as a proxy to application A.

Applications Linked by Complex Logic

At times, the logic needed to bind applications together is not of the type that can be addressed even by the previously described multi-step MSAI pattern. As you learned in the previous section, MSAI can link applications by means of sequential logical processing, but it cannot provide a means for complex logic such as a routing algorithm for delivery trucks that might be utilized by applications in a trucking company. This scenario requires that the custom logic is available as a service that other applications can participate in or be directed by.

Applications Unified Through User Interface

Although most of the integration discussed here occurs through writing intermediate code for server-to-server integration, it is certainly not restricted to that scenario specifically. Figure 3.5 depicts how two or more applications can be integrated via a common user interface. This is essentially the use of a client-side brokering application. The user interface does not need to be a *graphical user interface* (GUI) although more often than not, it is.

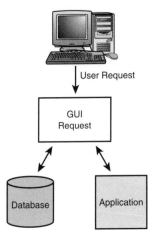

FIGURE 3.5

User interface–driven integration.

The use of this pattern is commonly applied in IT infrastructure as two-tiered client/server implementations. Implemented in this form, the unifying client-side application is a fat client accessing multiple databases or applications.

The Brokering Application pattern is used extensively even though it entails the writing of custom logic in part because there remains a class of problems that will only be solved by this pattern. This necessitates the use of technologies such as Application Servers, which will be described in greater detail in Chapter 5, "Application Servers."

Application-to-Application B2Bi

Now you're ready to move beyond EAI to learn about Application-to-Application B2Bi, extending integration beyond the corporate enterprise. I will describe four additional patterns related specifically to B2B integration, beginning first with the Application-to-Application B2Bi pattern. The Application-to-Application pattern is the logical extension of what occurs in EAI. When EAI vendors tout their products as being B2Bi, this specific pattern is what they have in mind. However, as you will discover, this is not the only pattern and very likely not even the primary pattern for B2Bi.

Application-to-Application B2Bi, which is often referred to as *inter-enterprise integration,* involves corporate entities linking their applications directly to the applications of their partners or customers, as shown in Figure 3.6. In practice, this type of integration is often implemented as part of a supply chain of goods and services to the customer.

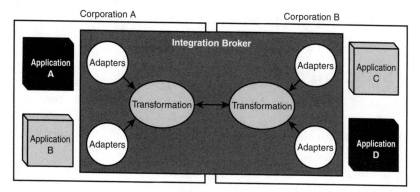

FIGURE 3.6
Application-to-Application B2Bi.

This picture does not imply that each application is entirely exposed. Only a subset of application data is externalized. The externalized application messages are the ones that are relevant to the partners or customers as part of the supply chain.

How is this pattern fundamentally different from application integration within the enterprise? As in enterprise integration, patterns such as the Multi-Step Application Integration pattern or the Brokering Application pattern may be applied. However, this pattern differs essentially from EAI in that it involves integration with external business entities, not simply applications. In this pattern, the applications are a direct *point of entry* into the business entity. This pattern will also likely require the use of a public network such as the Internet or a third-party network. This extension for inter-enterprise integration means that a number of additional issues need to be accounted for.

Security

The use of external networks and collaboration between external parties require a focus on security. Trust levels have to be established between participants. This means security measures have to be implemented for authentication, authorization, nonrepudiation, and secured data transport.

Federated Control

The issue of federated control means that each entity needs to be able to control elements of its own integration environment independently. However, it needs to be able to effectively participate in the common integration environment.

Systems Management

Finally, the management of the entire integration system needs to be addressed as well. Establishing the service-level agreements between the participants is essential for long-term success. This means that each participant signs up to ensure application availability and performance levels.

Data Exchange B2Bi

The limitation of the Application-to-Application B2Bi pattern is that it can be more demanding to implement. It necessitates that each participant handles and externalizes application native data directly. This makes it difficult to scale the B2B interaction model rapidly when such a demand is placed on the participants. The optimal solution is to provide a rapidly scalable B2Bi model in which participants can exchange data freely with minimal expectation on their infrastructure.

The Data Exchange B2Bi pattern enables B2B transactions predicated on a common data exchange format. It is the most widely applied pattern for B2B commerce today. Data Exchange B2Bi is effective because it is simple in concept and has been in use since the days of Electronic Data Interchange (EDI), the forerunner to today's B2B over the Internet.

Although there is a significant incumbency of legacy EDI transactions, the XML-based B2B will ultimately displace EDI as the primary mechanism for e-Business transactions. As Figure 3.7 illustrates, XML-based data packets are transmitted between two business entities through the use of a data exchange gateway service on both ends. One of the primary responsibilities of the gateway service is to prepare the data packets by placing them within a security envelope. The B2B gateway service supports security standards such as MIME, X.509, and S/Key. It is also responsible for routing data through a standard transport. Most B2B gateway services provide numerous transport options including HTTPS, FTP, and TCP/IP Sockets. However, upon examination, you will find that most B2Bi transactions still deliver XML documents over an HTTPS pipe.

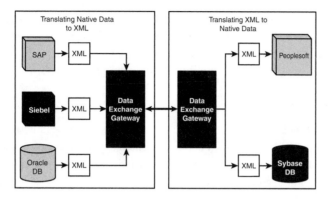

FIGURE 3.7
Data Exchange B2Bi.

A point to note with this pattern is that the interactions are still primarily point-to-point. Furthermore, the semantics of interaction (that is, the business processes) between the e-Business entities are static. Many trading standards have emerged to define both the content of document exchange as well as the common business processes. One such standard is promoted by an independent, nonprofit organization called RosettaNet. RosettaNet is committed to developing standard e-Business interfaces that cover, among other things, e-Business processes for standard business transactions. These process definitions are captured in what is known as *Partner Interface Processes*.

B2B Process Integration

Even with industrywide initiatives such as RosettaNet, a point-to-point data exchange that manages static interactions has some limitations. If Corporation A wants to purchase office supplies from Depot X, it must agree ahead of time on the content of the documents exchanged and buying process. This is, of course, to be expected. However, what if the situation involves managing multiple suppliers or if the interactions become more complex? For instance, a scenario in which suppliers openly bid to compete on pricing will increase the dimensions of process interactions. In that case, managing the B2B transaction is no longer an activity of managing a single point-to-point interaction. Instead, it becomes a challenge of managing business processes that are dynamic rather than static.

The B2B Process Integration pattern takes the limitations raised by the Data Exchange pattern and addresses them by providing Business Process Integration (BPI) services. Just as the Data Exchange pattern allows participants to manage data exchanges dynamically through XML-based documents, the B2B Process Integration pattern allows the participants to manage processes in the same way. Therefore, richer, more complex relationships can occur between trading partners.

3

E-BUSINESS INTEGRATION PATTERNS

B2B Process Integration pattern can be implemented as one of two variations: Closed Process B2Bi or Open Process B2Bi. You might argue that each of these variations constitutes an individual pattern, but because they share the common attribute of being process focused, I have decided to treat them as variations to the B2B Process Integration pattern.

Closed Process B2Bi

Closed Process B2Bi occurs when an organization manages processes internally and externalizes key process activities only through the data exchange gateway. Each organization through BPI is able to monitor the status of business process activities within the enterprise. Relevant business events are published to its partners through the data exchange gateway.

In Figure 3.8, Corporation A and Corporation B have both implemented BPI within the enterprise but have chosen not to directly expose these processes externally. Therefore, processes *between* the organizations are not managed. Instead, what exist are *two* sets of managed business processes linked together by a common gateway of published business events. The intra-enterprise implementation is at both the data and process level, whereas the inter-enterprise integration is purely at the data exchange level.

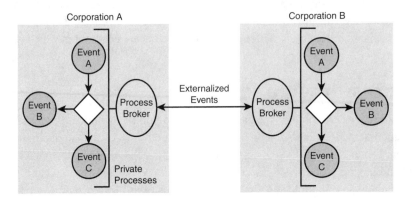

FIGURE 3.8
Closed Process B2Bi.

Open Process B2Bi

Open Process B2Bi creates the potential for sharing processes *between* multiple B2B corporate entities. Processes between companies are actually managed by both companies. This requires BPI products implemented by both corporate entities. Processes within the corporate walls can still be managed as *private* processes, limiting their visibility to within the corporate body. However, external B2B processes shared by both corporations are managed as public processes. The resulting picture should look something like Figure 3.9.

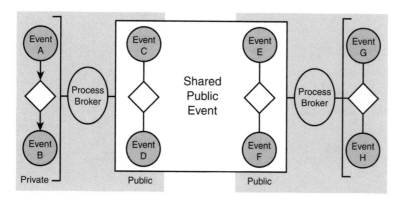

FIGURE 3.9
Open Process B2Bi

The Open Process B2Bi requires a BPI solution that allows for the segmenting of the management of public and private processes. Chapter 6, "Understanding Business Process Integration," discusses BPI in more detail.

Summary

This chapter introduced the concept of integration patterns. It also provided an integration pattern taxonomy, applied for both EAI as well as B2Bi. I covered the details behind seven primary integration patterns commonly applied today.

Chapter 4, "Integration Brokers," will introduce the first of the strategic e-Business Integration technologies: the integration broker. Integration brokers address the data integration layer and are used primarily, although not exclusively, within the enterprise. The chapter will discuss the fundamental attributes of the integration broker and explore how these attributes are critical to data integration. Chapter 4 will also provide a basis of evaluating integration brokers and assess some of the leading integration brokers on the market today.

e-Business Integration
Technologies

PART

II

IN THIS PART

Integration Brokers

"Everything should be as simple as it is, but not simpler."
—Albert Einstein

IN THIS CHAPTER

As I discussed briefly in Chapter 2, "e-Business Concepts and Architecture," the Data integration layer requires a set of services that accomplish more than simply moving data. An effective data integration solution needs to be able to translate, transform, and intelligently route data. You might be able to craft a solution by assembling a set of technologies to do just that. For instance, you may construct your integration solution by incorporating a transformation engine together with custom-coded application connectors and business rules. However, in recent years, a new technology has emerged to fulfill this specific need. All the necessary elements of data integration are encompassed in a single product offering. This product technology is known as the *integration broker*.

This chapter discusses how the integration broker evolved into its current form by providing a little historical perspective as well as describing its basic characteristics. The chapter also briefly covers the leading integration brokers on the market today.

Emergence of Integration Brokers

The idea of an integration broker as it is known today was originally introduced in a Gartner Group white paper authored by Roy Shulte, a leading Gartner analyst. In the Gartner white paper, this new integration technology was referred to as a *message broker*—a name that didn't always serve well because it often led to a mischaracterization. It was not unusual to observe confusion between true message brokers and Message Oriented Middleware (MOM) products that bear a similar name.

Although Mr. Shulte did not invent message brokers, he noted their existence and called attention to them as a key strategic technology for integration. Examples of message brokers in action were observed in vertical industries. In particular, the healthcare and financial sectors had applied fundamental message broker concepts for some time prior to 1996. Roy Shulte highlighted the need to take the vertically focused message broker and create a horizontal product solution. He raised awareness concerning the importance of message brokers in addressing the need for "intelligent" real-time transmission of data between corporate applications. This is primarily what Gartner referred to as the *zero latency enterprise* (ZLE). ZLE is the ideal of having the frictionless flow of information within corporate applications lending to availability and consistency of information.

More recently, message brokers have been known simply as *integration brokers*—a better name, if for no other reason than being self-descriptive. This technology will be referred to this way in this chapter as well as in the rest of the book.

Essential Elements of an Integration Broker

Because some integration brokers are based on message-oriented products such as the IBM MQ Series, assessing the fundamental differences of an integration broker can often be confusing. Is the integration broker merely a more "feature rich" messaging middleware, or do certain attributes comprise the definition of an integration broker? For integration brokers to be a distinctly different technology, it must have certain defined attributes. The following sections explore the essential attributes of integration brokers.

All integration brokers must share the following common elements:

- Robust document model
- Asynchronous messaging
- Content-based routing
- Data transformation
- Application interaction
- Graphically driven tools

Although each individual attribute is not unique to an integration broker, it is the composition of these attributes in a single product technology that uniquely defines the technology. Integration brokers may also possess other supporting functional elements that extend beyond this list, such as a repository service, Simple Network Management Protocol (SNMP) service, and version control. However, those extended functional elements do not essentially define an integration broker.

Robust Document Model

Integration brokers must implement a robust document model. It may not appear to be obvious at first, but the activity of integration begins and ends with the defined document or message model. (Note: The terms *message* and *document* are used interchangeably, but they essentially mean the same thing.) The integration document model is the canonical form, defining how data is structured and accessed *within* the integration broker architecture. It includes the data types, document layout, and methods that act on the document. By *robust*, I imply that the document model should be efficient, flexible, and functionally rich.

The document model should be efficient first and foremost with respect to the document size. This is particularly pertinent when you consider the need to place the document "on the wire;" that is, transport the document from point A to point B during the course of integrating. Without regard to the size of the document, precious network bandwidth will be inefficiently utilized transporting inordinately large application messages. SAP IDocs, for instance, are known to be exceedingly large.

The integration document model should also be flexible, allowing for the document to be easily extended to support complex formats such as those that use repeating data types or recursion. *Flexibility* also implies that it should accommodate change to the structure of the document with ease. When you keep this point in mind, this generally means that the document model should have self-describing attributes where the structure and constructs of the document are defined within the document itself.

Functional richness means that the document model must support methods used to access and manipulate the document. Beyond simply getting and setting data elements, it also includes the capability to browse through the document. It may also include advanced features such as the capability to filter data based on content. This capability has very practical implications with regard to integration. If a filter is applied, documents may be qualified before being placed on the wire to be transported for other integration activity. Figure 4.1 shows the conversion of application native data to integration document model.

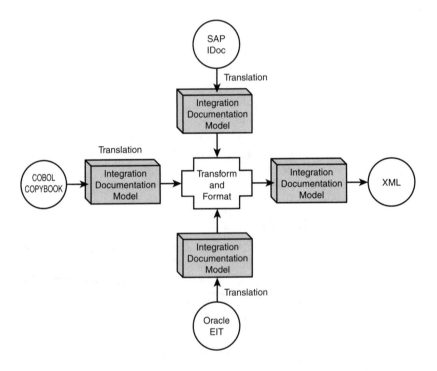

FIGURE 4.1

Application native data converted to the integration document model.

Although an integration broker can access various application messages through the use of adapters, most do not typically interact with those application messages in their native data form. Instead, the integration broker transforms, transports, and generally manipulates the data in terms of the common data form, the integration document model. Although the document model is a foundational element used by many components of the system, it is not acted on directly by the end user. In fact, the document model is actually transparent to the user of the integration broker. Furthermore, no industry standard document model is applied for integration brokers in general, with each product defining a proprietary model.

The lack of an industry standard raises the question—what about XML? Certainly, a few integration brokers have actually begun to adopt XML as the standard document model. However, for a number of valid reasons, the use of XML is often inadequate for an EAI solution. First, because XML is text based, it ends up being inefficient to use. The size of the document even when compressed leads to an inefficient use of network bandwidth as described previously. Furthermore, operations conducted on the document contents during the process of transformation require dealing with common data types such as integers or floats, especially in the case of mathematical computation. In these situations, the use of XML for the purposes of EAI is inefficient because it requires converting its text elements to these native data types such as integers or floats.

Consequently, some integration brokers package and transmit data in the form of a binary object. These objects have the benefit of being efficiently packaged, and the capability to deal with numeric data types during transformation provides a measure of efficiency in processing. Regardless of the document model selected, it is essential for that document model to adequately address the needs of an integration solution.

Asynchronous Messaging Service

When I say that integration brokers use asynchronous messaging, I am implying that the model for communication is fundamentally event based. Most integration brokers are primarily event based for a couple of reasons—one reason being mostly historical. Let's deal with the historical baggage first. Some of the older integration brokers actually evolved from a Message Oriented Middleware (MOM) heritage. MOM products began by fulfilling transport-level integration requirements by providing asynchronous messaging between two or more points. Later, many vendors added the capability to perform transformations as an extended feature, hence leading to the term *message broker*, forerunner to integration brokers today.

Asynchronous Messaging

Most asynchronous messaging is implemented in terms of a queuing or publish-subscribe messaging model, which will be explained in greater detail shortly. In either instance, the asynchronous messaging service acts as an intermediary delivery mechanism between client and server. In the integration of server-side applications, the source application acts as the client, and the target application is the server. The asynchronous messaging service provides message persistence at every messaging node. Figure 4.2 shows the asynchronous messaging server acting as an intermediary.

4

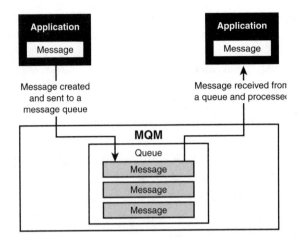

FIGURE 4.2

Asynchronous messaging server.

By relying on asynchronous messaging, integration brokers can provide the promise of "guaranteed message delivery." If the receiving target application is unable to process the message for any reason whatsoever, the asynchronous messaging server is responsible for the persistence of that message until the target application becomes available again.

Java Messaging Service

The Java Messaging Service (JMS) introduces an industry standard for messaging. Before JMS, messaging was proprietary based on each vendor's definition of terms and implementation of functionality. The JMS, a specification championed by Sun Microsystems, defines a messaging model for the industry. It is actually part of the Java 2 Enterprise Edition (J2EE) reference platform.

The JMS specification supports two messaging paradigms: point-to-point and publish-subscribe. Point-to-point messaging is enabled through the use of JMS queues. The JMS queue is a logical address for sending and receiving messages. It emulates synchronous behavior by having both a sending and receiving client exchange messages via an active connection to the queue. With a JMS queue, the receiving client reads messages destructively from the queue; that is, the messages are removed from the queue after being read.

Publish-subscribe works differently. It is predicated on a model in which multiple clients may be interested in the same message. A topic can have multiple publishers as well as multiple subscribers. A JMS topic is another logical mechanism like the queue used to manage message delivery. With the use of the topic, multiple clients can subscribe or listen on a topic. As a result, each listening client can receive the same message when a publisher client publishes to the topic.

Content-Based Routing

If there is something that classically illustrates the richness of integration brokers, it is the capability to perform *content-based routing* or, as it is sometimes referred to, *intelligent routing*. Content-based routing is a preferred descriptive term because it clearly defines the substance of what occurs. When messages are moved within a typical asynchronous messaging layer such as MQ Series or JMS, the message is placed into a logical queue or topic by the source application and is de-queued by the target application. The message is transported from source to destination based on a logical address. The Message Queuing Middleware has no "awareness" of the contents of the message, nor does it act on the message based on its contents. In this case, it is simply treated as a data packet to be transmitted.

With integration brokers, however, application messages are assessed, and message routing parameters such as priority and destination are governed by the contents of the message. This is accomplished by the application of rules within the integration broker. For instance, in Figure 4.3, the integration broker assesses the Customer_Order message. The contents are evaluated and rules are applied. Based on the rule "If the customer has purchased $100K worth of inventory year to date, the shipping charges are waived," the integration broker may set or transform the data before delivering target messages to the destination(s).

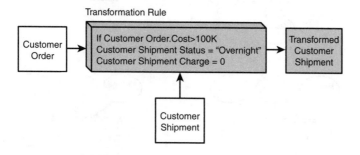

FIGURE 4.3

Content-based routing in action.

Content-based routing allows for intelligent mapping of data from source to destination. From the example, you have probably observed that the rules applied in integration brokers tend not to be "inference" or "artificial intelligent" rules but rather rules of sequential Boolean operations performed on data elements within the message.

4

Data Transformation

Data transformation is the very heart of what an integration broker does. The activity of data transformation is actually a combination of data translation and complex data formatting. Data translation involves the conversion of data syntax. Conversion of XML to SAP IDoc is an example of data translation. This entails placing the XML document and its Document Type Definition (DTD) as input into a translation framework that will result in SAP IDoc output documents. Another example may be the translation of XML into a binary object. The point with data translation is to perform conversions of data types or structure from one data form to another.

Data formatting is somewhat different from translation. It may initially appear to be a simple activity, but complex data formatting as performed by leading integration brokers actually enables mapping of messages in one-to-one, one-to-many, many-to-one, and many-to-many scenarios, as shown in Figure 4.4.

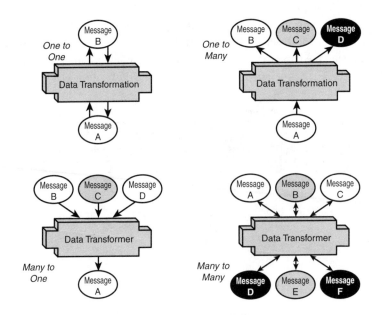

FIGURE 4.4

Complex data formatting scenarios.

One-to-one formatting involves a direct mapping of elements from message A to message B. The idea behind one-to-one formatting is simply that a single input message produces a single output message. Often the order, type, or size of data element may be radically altered, but the formatting does not result in multiple output messages. On the other hand, the one-to-many formatting requires the capability for the transformation facility to perform message splitting. Message splitting allows an input message to be split into multiple output messages. An example of message splitting is illustrated in Figure 4.5; here, a single Customer_order document with sections of multiple orders is split into *n* number of individual documents, each containing a single order.

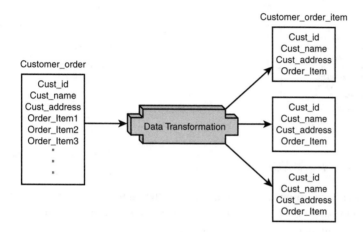

FIGURE 4.5

Message splitting.

The converse of message splitting occurs where multiple messages are combined into a single message as in the many-to-one scenario. Message combining is the capability of the transformation engine to receive multiple input messages, possibly from different sources, and to format the data into a single output message. A practical example of this may occur where multiple Customer_orders entered on the same day may be consolidated into a single shipping order rather than shipping multiple packages.

Many-to-many transformation is the most complex form in which multiple input messages are formatted into multiple output messages. In many integration brokers, instead of a single schema mapping function enabling mapping from multiple input documents to multiple output documents, it is accomplished in a two-phased process. It can be accomplished by chaining together the many-to-one mapping to the one-to-many mapping, as shown in Figure 4.6.

4

INTEGRATION BROKERS

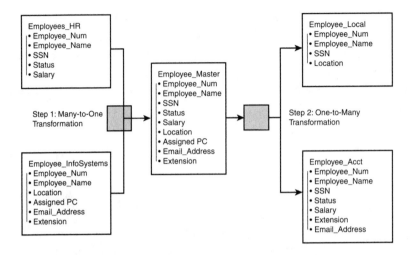

FIGURE 4.6

Chaining many to one and one to many.

The output of the many-to-one conversion provides the input into the one-to-many conversion. Although this approach may be assessed as inefficient, it is essentially equivalent in a practical sense and is used widely by many integration brokers.

Application Interaction

Integration brokers were conceived to address the problem of application integration. The capability to connect to applications is paramount to accomplishing that objective. Most integration brokers provide adapters—components that can interact with the application or data resource. This interaction includes inserting, updating, extracting, or receiving application data. The delete function is seldom supported because with integration there is typically little need for deletion of data.

When integration broker vendors speak of adapters, it is important to recognize that no single standard defines an adapter. Adapters vary from vendor to vendor, depending on the level of functional sophistication involved. Depending on functional capacity, adapters can address the broad need for application interaction in three different ways, as described in the following three sections.

Session Management

Session management equates to the capability to interface with the application through a managed connection for the duration of time or activity. This means being able to provide data connectivity, access, and protocol. When it comes to adapting to applications, connectivity is ground zero. Connectivity establishes a communication channel with the application. It permits data to flow between the adapter and application. Adapters are also responsible for interfacing with the application logic and data. This may be accomplished through various mechanisms. They include direct access to the application database or programmable application interfaces provided by some applications. This topic will be covered in greater depth in Chapter 9, "Using Adapters for Application Data Access."

Data Management

Data management is very broad term with design-time as well as runtime implications. During design time, it refers to application meta-data extraction and application schema mapping. Adapter design components are able manage the application meta data. This includes extraction as well as versioning of meta data. Schema management allows for application elements to be mapped to a defined message. At runtime, the adapter is responsible for accessing and retrieving the application data. It also performs the runtime mapping of the actual application data elements to the predefined message.

Node-Level Processing

Adapters function as an outer node in the traditional hub-spoke architecture. Typically, in this architecture, most of the processing of filtering and data transformation occurs within the hub. Some of the more advanced adapters provide the capability to filter and even transform at the node level. Figure 4.7 illustrates how node-level processing works.

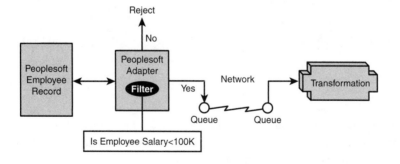

FIGURE 4.7
Node-level processing by adapters.

Instead of placing every message "on the wire" to be processed by the transformation hub, the advanced adapters can qualify the data at runtime based on filters applied at the node level. The functional capability is then pushed to the nodes, leading to increased efficiency and scalability. Adapters that can perform this level of processing are often called *agent-adapters*.

4

INTEGRATION
BROKERS

Graphically Driven Tools

Strictly speaking, the provision of a graphical tool is not an essential part of the integration broker infrastructure. Instead the essential element is a focus on the use of graphically driven methods to accomplish integration. Instead of an inherently programming-centric approach, integration brokers provide tools to graphically define what can best be described as an integration data flow. An example of a data integration flow is shown in Figure 4.8.

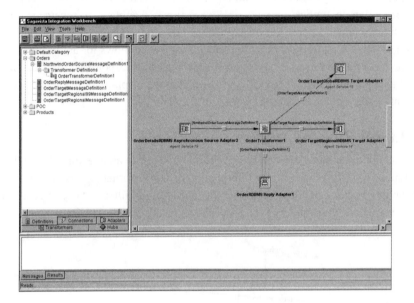

FIGURE 4.8
Data integration flow.

Rather than integrate via coding-intensive methods, the user can define the data integration flow, enabling the flow of data between applications. Tasks such as the extraction of application meta data, the definition of mappings, and transformation operations can be defined graphically.

Integration Broker Runtime Architecture

Now that you understand the requisite characteristics of an integration broker, the following discussion delves into how they actually work. The first point to understand is that no standard architecture exists for integration broker technology. Each vendor takes an individual approach to crafting its product architecture. With an absence of standardization, each product works in different ways. Now that I've said that, what follows is a basic reference model for integration broker runtime architecture based on the fundamental characteristics discussed in the previous section. Although some older integration brokers do not conform to this reference architecture, newer integration brokers are based on this distributed, component-based model. And increasingly, the need for scalable integration calls for its adoption. Distributed integration brokers are made up of the components described in the following five sections.

Repository

The repository provides storage of design-time message definitions, integration flow configurations, and persisted objects. In some of the more advanced integration brokers, a repository service provides an interface for accessing and managing the stored objects and configurations. The actual physical persistence of these objects and configurations is handled by a relational database.

Transformation Engine

The transformation engine provides translation and formatting of messages from one or more sources. It also may be associated with a rules facility, enabling data conversion or sequential Boolean logic to be applied as part of the transformation. Hence, the transformation engine often encapsulates the functional components of translation, formatting, filtering, and rules.

Routing Hub

The routing hub is responsible for high-speed delivery of messages to the target destinations. It is particularly efficient for one-to-many or many-to-many integration. After the resulting message has been transformed by the transformation engine and is ready for delivery, the routing hub sorts and delivers the message(s) to the appropriate destinations.

Messaging Service

The messaging service should provide the transport mechanism for the integration broker. It should support both publish-subscribe as well as point-to-point message queuing. Additionally, it should not be restricted to just asynchronous messaging but also provide support for integration components to utilize synchronous facilities such as Remote Method Invocation (RMI) or Remote Procedure Call (RPC).

Adapters

Adapters provide application connectivity. At runtime, adapters can extract and insert data into applications via a variety of mechanisms. Advanced adapters also allow for filtering and limited rules to be applied before transporting the message to the transformation engine.

The distributed integration broker architecture is made up of these components working together to provide scalable integration. Figure 4.9 illustrates how the various components of the integration broker architecture function at runtime.

4

INTEGRATION
BROKERS

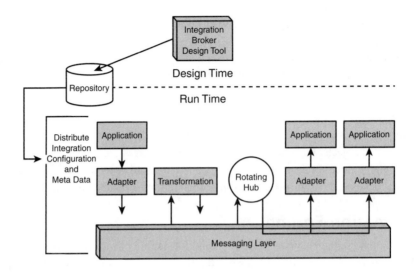

FIGURE 4.9

Integration broker runtime.

The operational sequence for an integration broker is defined by the primary steps below. It describes the specific sequences for component start-up, application connectivity and integration logic.

1. At startup, the components load the integration meta data from the repository. This includes physical configuration parameters as well as integration meta data. Physical configuration parameters include information for the adapters such as port addresses or database connection information. The integration meta data refers to transformations, rules, or filters applied to a given integration data flow. It also includes data schema mappings.

2. Based on the related integration meta data, each component registers with the messaging layer, subscribing to the appropriate topic or queue. Simultaneously, adapters also establish a direct connection with the source or target applications. Source adapters are either in a polling mode or listening mode, depending on the nature of the application concerned. If the application has an event-based mechanism for application message retrieval, it is generally regarded as preferable to a polling model.

3. As the adapters receive application messages, filters may be applied before the message is published into a queue.

4. The transformation engine is subscribed to the queue. It receives the message and processes it based on predefined parameters. This means invoking defined translation, formatting, and conversion elements. It also includes incorporating other messages in a

many-to-one or many-to-many scenario. The resulting output messages for a given integration flow are filtered and delivered by the routing engine to the appropriate queues. At times, this routing hub may be part of the messaging layer.

5. The adapters de-queue the output messages and insert them into the target applications to complete the integration flow.

Leading Integration Brokers

Before you embark into this section, a little disclaimer and disclosure are in order. First, in this section, I am not attempting to cover every integration broker in the market. I have selected a cross section of four different integration brokers covering, in broad strokes, background information as well as perceived strengths and weaknesses. Each product has a distinctly different emphasis that I will attempt to draw out in the discussion. Second, it is impossible to address the details of each integration broker product in a couple of paragraphs, and I do not pretend to try. Treat this discussion as an overview of integration broker products and how they generally compare but not as point-for-point in-depth research on each product.

Finally, in the interest of complete disclosure, my coauthor and I are most familiar with Sagavista from SAGA Software because we played key roles in designing the product. However, I believe that you will find the treatment of all the products to be fair and unbiased. This is in keeping with the foremost intent of this book—to serve the audience with valuable information about e-Business Integration technology.

The following sections explore integration brokers from these leading companies:

- New Era of Networks (NEON)
- SAGA Software
- STC
- webMethods-Active Software

New Era of Networks

New Era of Networks (NEON) is one of the leading vendors in the e-Business Integration market segment. It boasts more than 1,000 customers and has established its position through aggressive acquisitions of technology and services companies. The center of the NEON product offering is e-Biz Integrator, which is essentially an integration broker, providing application connectivity, data transformations, and synchronization of corporate data.

NEON identifies three primary areas of functionality supplied by e-Biz Integrator: message queuing, formatting, and rules. e-Biz Integrator's message queuing is, as expected, typically asynchronous with guaranteed message delivery. The e-Biz Integrator Formatter is a component that provides dynamic message formatting. It can perform the many-to-many formatting required for complex environments. It is able to translate between XML to multiple legacy and package application messages. The e-Biz Integrator also includes a Rules Engine that enables the delivery of context-relevant message content to target systems.

In addition to e-Biz Integrator, NEON offers a set of adapters that can address integration with ERP systems and industry standards such as EDI, ACORD, FIX, and SWIFT. In particular, based on NEON's heritage and success in the financial industry, its adapter for the Society for Worldwide InterBank Financial Telecommunication, or SWIFT, is notably strong.

SAGA Software

SAGA Software is the newest entrant in the integration broker space with its award-winning integration broker, Sagavista. With version 1.0 released in September 1999, Sagavista is a distributed Java integration broker built around open standards such as Java Messaging Service (JMS), Java Native Directory Interface(JNDI), Java Database Connectivity (JDBC), and XML.

One of Sagavista's primary strengths is its ease of use. The Integration Workbench provides a graphical wizard-driven development of an integration flow. With little programming, the user can put together a complex integration flow by mapping data elements and defining transformations. Distinguished by its adapter technology, Sagavista allows rapid end-to-end development of the integration flow. As you learned earlier, often the most challenging part of integration is addressing the point of interface with the application. Sagavista excels here with its adapters that allow for the extraction and management of application meta data. Its adapters allow filtering of application messages at the nodes, preventing unnecessary placement of data on the network. SAGA plans J2EE Connector Architecture support for its adapters.

Sagavista is also strong architecturally. Its runtime distributed architecture is made up of multiple instances of adapters, transformers, and rule functions. Its latest release also provides component load-balancing service. Sagavista's messaging is based on the JMS standard. Although it is packaged with a default JMS messaging server, Sagavista can support most JMS messaging providers. It is an example of the open standards that Sagavista is known for.

Sagavista also leverages its 100% Java architecture in another way. It affords close interoperability with application servers through specialized e-Business adapters. These e-Business adapters allow component requests to be issued as execution of integration flows that return the correlated result set.

STC

STC may be the grandfather of the integration broker vendors. The company has a mature product line with a strong hold in the healthcare sector. It has broadened its product to address far more than the healthcare vertical. STC's flagship product is e*Gate, which it positions as an e-Business Integration platform.

e*Gate is an integration broker with a distributed architecture. The administration of e*Gate is conducted by management components known as the Registry and Control Brokers. The Registry retains a master copy of all parameterized data, and the Control Brokers manage the configuration changes to the distributed components. e*Gate also represents data transformations, rules, and routing logic as a fundamental element known as a *collaboration*. Collaborations are expressed by a proprietary scripting language and can be manipulated through the use of a Collaboration Editor tool.

e*Gate's transport layer uses the publish-subscribe messaging model. It also supports other third-party messaging products such as the IBM MQ Series. There are also adapters that provide application connectivity to databases (for example, Oracle, Sybase), packaged applications (for example, SAP, Peoplesoft, Clarify), and legacy systems (for example, CICS, IMS).

webMethods

webMethods, known for B2B integration, extended its capability by acquiring Active Software. Active Software's product line, ActiveWorks, was renamed and recast as webMethods Enterprise products. The heart of the product line is the webMethods Enterprise Broker, which functions as an integration broker with reliable message delivery, transformations, and rules. Accompanying the Enterprise Broker is a set of development and management productivity tools. The webMethods Enterprise tools include the Visual Integrator, Business Integrator, and Application Transaction Coordinator.

The Visual Integrator allows the user to construct an integrated solution rapidly by graphically defining integration units that are part of an integration process. After these integration units are defined, the user connects the units together. In addition to this tool, webMethods also offers a Business Integrator product, which approaches the integration problem by allowing the user to model logical business processes. It also allows the user to define transformations and other quality-of-service elements such as error handling, logging, and statistics. Finally, the Application Transaction Coordinator provides management of long-running transactions that span multiple applications. It ensures that messages are tracked and managed from end to end. webMethods also provides more than 50 adapters to many applications, databases, and industry standards.

Summary

This chapter examined the details behind the integration broker technology. The emergence of integration brokers as the next evolution of data integration technology was discussed. This chapter also presented six defining attributes of an integration broker:

- Robust document model
- Asynchronous messaging

4

INTEGRATION BROKERS

- Content based routing
- Data transformation
- Application interaction
- Graphical driven tools

Chapter 5, "Application Servers," will explore one of the most compelling technologies today—the application server. The chapter will define the application server by an examination of its core attributes. No discussion of application servers will be complete without attention to the emerging Java 2 Enterprise Edition (J2EE) platform. You will spend some time delving into the primary J2EE services and the role they play in integration.

Application Servers

"The Internet revolution will make the PC revolution look pale in comparison."
—Ed Zander, president and COO of Sun Microsystems

IN THIS CHAPTER

Application server technology has been the hidden engine enabling the expansion of e-Business. Leading analysts predict that application servers will be center stage for a number of years. In fact, GIGA Information Group released research data anticipating growth of the application server market to reach $9 billion by 2003. Application servers, a relatively new player in the middleware category, allow for enterprise application resources (that is, business logic and data) to be accessed and managed in a consistent fashion. This chapter explores the application server technology and examines its use in e-Business Integration. It also highlights four leading application servers on the market today.

Application servers also play a vital role in e-Business Integration, as you learned in Chapter 3, "e-Business Integration Patterns," on integration patterns. The Brokering Application pattern uses intermediary application logic to broker information between enterprise applications. Instead of simple sharing of data, this pattern addresses scenarios in which it is necessary to share application logic that binds diverse applications together. The intermediary application in this pattern is actually custom-coded integration logic accessing, transforming, and transporting application data from one application to another.

How Application Servers Emerged

Application servers have really emerged from the evolution of client/server. Early implementations of client/server were of the two-tier variety. This first generation client/server architecture called for application logic to be primarily embedded in the client. The client segment was responsible for both the presentation as well as business processing. The server portion of the application typically constituted a SQL database hosting business data. Although this approach promised benefits of decentralization, the two-tier client/server model shown below in Figure 5.1 proved too limited in its capability to scale.

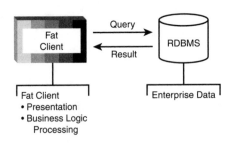

FIGURE 5.1

Two-tier client/server.

This limitation led to the evolution toward multitier client/server computing models. Most modern client/server architectures allow for multiple tiers with presentation, business logic, and business data layers. In the multitier client/server model, like the two-tier client/server architecture, business data is hosted by a back-end database server. However, unlike the two-tier model, the multitier client/server system employs a "thin client" to address the presentation layer. The business or application logic is encapsulated in a middle tier. Multitier client/server systems lead to more performance, scalability, and portability than their two-tier counterparts. However, implementing the middle tier can be technically challenging, with complex code needed to provide supporting services such as a distributed component model, session management, transaction processing, and security.

Multitier Client/Server

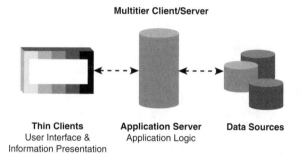

Thin Clients	Application Server	Data Sources
User Interface & Information Presentation	Application Logic	

FIGURE 5.2
Multitier client/server architectures.

That's where the application server comes in. Instead of reinventing the wheel each time, the developer can leverage the services provided by the application server to host, manage, and secure the business logic tier. And as distributed computing architectures grow in complexity, other services will be needed. Eventually, the notion of an application server will be extended to meet the need for new application services such as those for Web transactions and mobile computing.

What Exactly Is an Application Server?

So far, I've covered what application servers do without really defining the basic characteristics of application servers. As it turns out, defining them is no easy task. The fact is that there is no such thing as a standard application server. Each application server may differ depending on the functional services it supports. In essence, an application server is simply a collection of services that support the development, runtime execution, and management of business logic. In practice, this means that what may seem like a single application server is actually a collection of servers with application-related services. Under these rather broad definitions, application servers include

Microsoft's AppCenter as well as many of the Java-based application servers such as BEA WebLogic. In general, however, the term *application server* primarily refers to Java-based application servers. In this chapter and throughout this book, when I speak of application servers, my primary reference points are the many Java-based application servers on the market.

Although no reference implementation model exists for application servers, most products attempt to provide tools and services that address the following objectives:

- Execution of business logic
- High performance
- Scalability
- High availability
- Security management
- Transaction management
- Systems management
- Development tools and services

If you are selecting an application server, you can also use these points as a basis for evaluation.

Execution of Business Logic

The fundamental purpose of application servers is to provide a platform of services to execute business logic. This means providing a hosting service for business logic components. These components may take the form of servlets or Enterprise Java Beans (EJB) components. In either case, the application server's primary responsibility is to execute these components when invoked at runtime by a client request.

High Performance

An application server does more than simply execute business logic. It provides facilities to ensure that the business logic is executed to high performance characteristics. It does so by providing performance enhancement services such as connection pooling, multithreading, and caching.

Scalability

Scalability can often be misconstrued. Many discussions on scalability quickly digress to performance, but strictly speaking scalability is a separate element of a system's characteristics. Whereas performance addresses throughput and execution speed, scalability refers to the capability to support an increasing volume of client requests without degradation. One way by which application servers address the need for horizontal scalability (that is, the capability to add additional servers to support increasing client requests) is through providing a clustering service. The clustering service depicted in Figure 5.3 provides the facility to manage and partition workload. Multiple copies of business components can be instantiated and run simultaneously. As client requests come in, the clustering service synchronizes and distributes the requests to be fulfilled by each component.

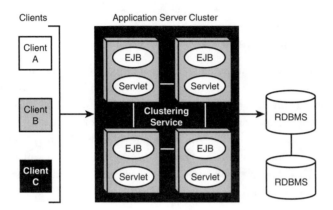

FIGURE 5.3

A clustering service managing a workload.

High Availability

Clustering also guarantees high availability by eliminating single points of failure. Client requests to unavailable or unresponsive components automatically fail-over to an available component. This fail-over sequence should be managed transparently to the requester.

Security Management

Application server products seek to provide a unified and comprehensive security architecture. Instead of having to piece together a security model based on various technologies, the developer uses a consistent set of services provided by the application server. The security elements that are addressed include authentication, authorization, and secured transport.

Authentication ensures that the identity of the client is valid, whereas authorization addresses the boundaries of access and permissions. Transport can be secured through the use of technologies such as the Secure Socket Layer (SSL).

Transaction Management

Although transaction management is not inherently a necessary application server functionality, an increasing number of application servers provide it as a service. More established application servers leverage existing transactional management technologies, whereas newer application servers leverage the emerging Java Transaction API (JTA) standard in providing the functionality.

Systems Management

Application servers promote a distributed component-based model for computing. Although multitier distributed systems have many advantages, they are inherently difficult to deploy and manage. Systems management services such as the capability to start and stop business components, monitor availability, and track performance are not optional "nice to have" features but are essential to the successful execution. Application servers should provide the capability to support the Simple Network Management Protocol (SNMP) standard for management of application components. This way, the application can be managed by leading systems management tools such as HP OpenView, IBM Tivoli, or BMC Patrol.

Development Tools and Services

Application servers ease the development of scalable, modular application code by offering integrated development environment (IDE) tools or tools that plug into existing IDEs. The developer is given a choice of language bindings and a complementary set of tools that may include compiler(s), class libraries, sample applications, as well as debugging and testing facilities.

Application Servers and the J2EE Platform

Java 2 Enterprise Edition (J2EE), launched and promoted by Sun Microsystems since June 1999, provides a Java-based reference platform for developing and integrating enterprise applications. Since that time, the momentum behind this standard platform has only increased exponentially. Instead of each application server vendor designing and implementing enterprise services in a proprietary fashion, the J2EE platform ensures that these services will be available and accessed under a standard architectural framework.

J2EE is first and foremost a reference architectural model for developing component-based applications. It is predicated on a view of applications in a multitier distributed computing model made up of clients, Web services, enterprise component services, and data access services. The J2EE architecture is depicted in Figure 5.4 below.

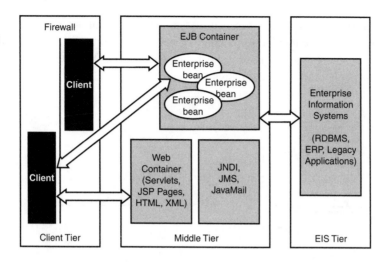

FIGURE 5.4
J2EE architecture.

Numerous types of clients are supported in this model, ranging from fat client applications to thin clients running browsers on wireless handheld devices. The Web services tier provides container services for primarily Web-based elements such as Java servlets and Java Server Pages (JSP). The enterprise component service tier revolves around the EJB container that enables EJB components to be hosted. Other supporting services to leverage the management of EJB components are part of this layer. The data access tier is commonly referred to in J2EE vernacular as the enterprise information systems (EIS) tier.

The EJB Component Model

The EJB component model, in simplistic terms, consists of the enterprise component and the runtime environment that surrounds that component known as the *container*. This is shown in Figure 5.5. The container provides a set of standard facilities for EJB component life-cycle management, persistence, and database access. Strictly speaking, the container is not the run-time server process but rather a defined environment that executes and manages the component. The server is a physical runtime entity that encompasses the container.

EJB components, generically known as *beans,* come in two flavors: session beans and entity beans.

Session beans model units of work or sessions. To put it another way, session beans contain business processing logic like calculations or the flow of activity. Session beans can also be *stateful* or *stateless* in nature. Stateful session beans maintain a conversational mode with the client. This means the client is always aware of the state of the component. Between client invocations of a method, the state of variables within the component is maintained. Stateless beans, when invoked by a client, perform a unit of work with results passed back to the client. The state of the component is not preserved between method calls because there is no obligation to maintain an ongoing conversation with the client.

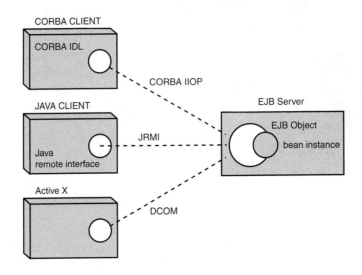

FIGURE 5.5
The EJB component model.

Entity beans, on the other hand, model business data. For instance, an entity bean may correlate to a customer object or an inventory database record. One of the primary roles of the EJB container is to manage persistence on behalf of the entity bean. However, an entity bean may also be developed to manage its own persistence, independent of the container. This is known as *bean-managed persistence*.

J2EE Standard Services

Besides providing an architectural model for component-based applications, J2EE can also be viewed as a collection of standards for enterprise services. These standard services include the following:

- **Java Naming and Directory Service (JNDI)** provides a standard Java API for naming and directory services. Client applications may search for objects by attributes. JNDI providers for existing directory services such as DNS, LDAP, and NDS are readily available.

- **Java Database Connectivity API (JDBC)** is also part of the J2EE standard API set. JDBC may be the most widely adopted of J2EE standards and is in use by many applications for database access.

- **Java Messaging Service (JMS)** provides a standard Java-based messaging model and API. It has been widely adopted as well by existing messaging systems such as MQ Series. JMS supports two primary messaging models: publish-subscribe and point-to-point messaging. Publish-subscribe messaging allows users to publish anonymously to a node where subscribers to that node may receive the message. Point-to-point messaging delivers the message from the sender directly to the queue of the receiver.

- **Java Transaction API (JTA)** specifies standard interoperability between the client, transactional application, or system and the transaction manager. For an existing transaction manager like Tuxedo to support J2EE, it would have to provide transaction management interfaces that conform to JTA. JTS is a specification that defines the implementation of a JTA transaction manager.

- **J2EE Connector Architecture**, the most recent addition to the J2EE standards, provides an API for accessing EIS or enterprise applications. Examples of EIS include transactional mainframe systems, ERP applications, and corporate databases. It provides standards for managing application connectivity, encompassing elements such as connection pooling, security, and error handling. The notion is that clients can access applications through a standard client interface while EIS systems can externalize data through a common mechanism. Because this topic has significance for adapters, it will be covered in Chapter 9, "Using Adapters for Application Data Access."

The J2EE platform is significant because it provides a framework for application server providers to conform to. Instead of numerous proprietary implementations and architectural models, basic services can be provided through a common component model. This leads to faster development and deployment of Java-based applications. What isn't covered by the J2EE standard? Key functional elements such as clustering, load balancing, and systems management services are among the functional elements that aren't covered. However, there are also opportunities for each application server to innovate and distinguish themselves from the competition.

Using Application Servers for Integration

Application servers can be used for integration in various ways, most notably in two basic patterns. The first pattern uses application servers primarily in the intermediary application logic model, as discussed in Chapter 3. It uses JDBC for database access and adapters for application access. In the near future, as more application servers conform to the J2EE connector architecture, it will be deployed in the form shown in Figure 5.6.

5

APPLICATION SERVERS

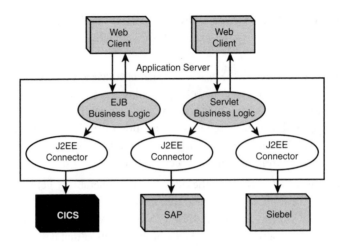

FIGURE 5.6

Application servers with J2EE connectors.

The limitation behind this approach is that access to enterprise data is synchronous, dependent on a one-to-one connection with the applications, and it requires custom-coded application integration logic. This is not a problem when two or even three applications are integrated. However, it rapidly becomes a problem as more applications are brought online to be integrated. If the custom integration logic in place does not support the new applications, further coding is required. This approach to "hard-wire" integration logic is limited in its capability to extend the number and types of applications supported. On the other hand, application server technology is viable and even preferable when common complex logic is shared between applications. Application servers fit the bill in instances in which complex application logic, commonly shared between application modules, becomes the basis of integration. For instance, a just-in-time inventory system and shipping program might share the use of a ship routing algorithm that results in the integration of data from both these sources. An application server would host the ship routing logic shared by both applications and facilitate the passing of information between both applications.

However, other classes of integration problems necessitate a more flexible and dynamic tool. Integration brokers are simply more effective for data-level integration problems. Integration at this layer involves mostly data mapping, transformation, and logical rules of evaluation.

Application servers can also be used in tandem with integration brokers through a cooperative interface. By using both application servers and integration brokers together, you get the best of both worlds. Figure 5.7 illustrates this cooperative model between application servers and integration brokers.

Incorporating the use of integration brokers provides two benefits. First, the integration broker functions as an intelligent application integration backbone while the application server hosts custom business logic in the middle tier. In this mode, it functions as a service provider to the application server by providing data access, transformations, and content-based routing. The second advantage of this model is that the integration broker can provide a virtual consolidated view of the enterprise data. Although integration brokers are not usually thought of in this fashion, the integration broker is able to externalize virtual business objects that are essentially composite messages based on various applications messages.

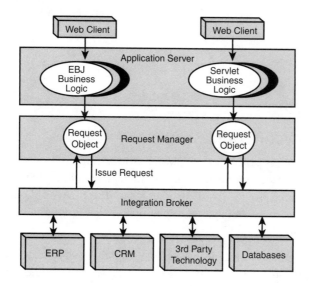

FIGURE 5.7

Application servers and integration brokers together.

The client makes a request to a session bean hosted by the application server. If the request necessitates access and integration at the data level, the request is passed into the integration broker through an intermediate software element known as the *request manager*. The integration broker then services that request, which, in some cases, may be simply a request to a single data resource. However, more complex requests require the integration broker to combine the information from multiple application sources before returning the results to the application server.

The challenge in this model is resolving the application server's synchronous component method calls with the asynchronous messaging-based integration broker. When a component makes a method call to retrieve data, it typically (although not always) expects the request and subsequent reply to be marshaled over a synchronous channel. A link exists between the request and the reply. When the integration broker is used to retrieve the data, no such one-to-one link exists. Instead, the request is channeled through the request manager component. The request manager is responsible for correlating request messages placed into a queue and its corresponding result set that may be delivered to another queue.

Overview of Leading Application Servers

Just as the preceding chapter profiled the leading integration brokers, this chapter highlights four leading application servers. Each application server may differ in the peripheral services offered, but all four provide basic services for runtime component execution, security, systems management, and scalable services. The four application servers profiled are as follows:

- BEA WebLogic
- IBM WebSphere
- SUN iPlanet
- HP-Bluestone Sapphire

BEA Systems WebLogic Server

Founded in 1996, BEA has experienced explosive growth, initially focusing on transaction management with the Tuxedo product. From that foundation, it has established itself as the leading application server provider on the market today. The BEA WebLogic Server (WLS) currently leads the pack in providing a set of platform services for building J2EE-based e-Business applications.

BEA WLS provides services to enable application scalability and high availability. It does so through its strength in clustering services. The clustering service provides component replication, load balancing, and fail-over capability. Component replication means that multiple copies of a business component may be instantiated to accommodate multiple simultaneous requests. Load balancing generally refers to the partitioning of a workload in a dynamic fashion, allowing for management of "high and low watermarks"; that is, with a "high watermark," when the workload reaches a certain level, a new component is replicated and work is channeled to that component. Fail-over ensures that requests to a particular EJB component are dynamically transferred to another EJB component in the event that the first component fails or is unavailable. The idea is that the request should never be permitted to fail.

BEA also provides a complementary set of tools through WebGain, its tools subsidiary. WebGain tools are among the best in the market, with Visual Café and a set of add-on tools. WLS also works with other leading tools such as IBM Visual Age and Inprise JBuilder. BEA WLS also serves as the foundation for additional products in the BEA family, such as WebLogic Process Integrator and WebLogic Collaborator.

Bluestone Software Sapphire

Often you can measure leaders only in terms of market share and ignore other technical parameters. That approach may leave out smaller players that lead in technical strength but fail to establish leadership through possible deficiencies in market positioning. Bluestone Software would be an example of such a company. Bluestone Software provides elements of what it has defined as the complete e-Business Platform to include infrastructure, integration, content management, personalization, electronic commerce, and wireless integration. This broad offering may mask a distinct strength in infrastructure services. Although Sapphire is not a transaction monitor, it manages state through its Internet Quality of Service (IQS) facility. This allows the state of a request to be managed and fine-grained control over how requests are serviced. Bluestone Sapphire also has a proven capability to manage workload through the Load Balance Broker (LBB) component in the Sapphire architecture. The LBB manages load via a number of mechanisms, including a method known as Burst-Mode Optimization that manages and optimizes unusual spikes in load processing. The Universal Business Server provides an EJB container as well as host services to execute Java Server Pages (JSP).

Bluestone Software also recently extended Sapphire's capability as a transactional platform with its acquisition of Arjuna, a small company in the UK specializing in distributed transactions. This acquisition enables Bluestone Software to incorporate transaction management capability into its application server offering. The transactional services support the Java Transaction API (JTA). At the time of writing, Hewlett Packard is in the process of acquiring Bluestone Software which would provide broader opportunities for this technically strong product.

IBM WebSphere

IBM WebSphere is really a three-tiered family of application servers: Standard Edition, Advanced Edition, and Enterprise Edition. Most of the discussion in reference to WebSphere will center on the Advanced and Enterprise Editions.

WebSphere provides an environment for building, deploying, and managing application logic. Although WebSphere has been slower to adopt the J2EE architecture in its product offering, it nonetheless is made up of an EJB server. The EJB server is responsible for managing EJB components through an EJB container. The EJB server also provides supporting services for thread pooling, transactional support, and data management. The WebSphere Administration Console provides centralized management of components within the WebSphere environment. The administration model within WebSphere allows for the organization of a domain known as a *managed node*. A managed node consists of an administration console and a collection of individual machines running WebSphere resources. WebSphere resources include EJB components, EJB containers, JSP, and Java servlets.

WebSphere Enterprise Edition includes all the Advanced Edition features as well as the Component Broker and TX Series products. Component Broker is a distributed enterprise middleware product based on CORBA. Component Broker also supports EJB by providing its own implementation of an EJB container. The TX Series includes transactional components with CICS and Encina. Both products offer services to construct highly available and scalable transactional applications.

SUN-Netscape Alliance iPlanet

Like most of the application servers mentioned, iPlanet is actually more than an application server. It is actually a family of products for which the iPlanet Application Server is the base product. iPlanet Application Server allows the user to develop J2EE-based applications and provides services for reliability, scalability, and integration.

The iPlanet Application Server minimizes single points of failure through multilevel application fail-over service for EJB and JSP. It can perform state management over multiple servers. It provides additional facilities that boost performance and system throughput such as connection pooling, caching of connections and results, as well as multithreading. The Unified Integration Framework provides a set of classes and a meta-data repository oriented to solving integration problems.

The iPlanet Application Server is tightly integrated with a number of tools, including the iPlanet Application Builder, Forte for Java, and even third-party tools such as IBM Visual Age. iPlanet Application Builder is the complementary development tool that allows the user to develop via a wizard-driven approach.

Summary

Absent an industry standard definition, the application server has really not been defined as a technology. This chapter explained in detail the basic services of an application server. It also provided a context for understanding the technology. It also examined the emerging J2EE platform standard. J2EE is already becoming the de-facto enterprise component standard. I also discussed other key standards in the J2EE model such as JMS, JNDI and JDBC.

Chapter 6, "Understanding Business Process Integration," will explore another technology vital to e-Business Integration—the Business Process Integration (BPI) engine. Users can experience a great deal of confusion about what BPI technology is and how it works in conjunction with other integration technologies. This chapter will dispel misconceptions about BPI and engage in a discussion about BPI functional elements.

Understanding Business Process Integration

"Everything that can be invented has been invented."
—Charles H. Duell, Commissioner, U.S. Office of Patents, 1899

IN THIS CHAPTER

Industry experts are waking up to the fact that Business Process Integration (BPI) is the essential enabler for a scalable e-Business Integration infrastructure. Many products previously in the workflow space have been recast in this emerging BPI market. Further evidence of its importance is confirmed by the introduction of new products from major vendors such as Microsoft (Biztalk) and BEA (Weblogic Process Integrator) that specifically address BPI.

Yet, despite the acknowledgment regarding its importance, this technology is still not well understood. Often, the introduction of other technologies, such as integration brokers and document workflow products, only serves to blur the BPI picture. I believe this chapter will go a long way toward clarifying what BPI is all about; its primary functionality and architecture. It will provide you with an understanding of BPI, not simply as an independent technology but as a piece of the overall suite of e-Business Integration technologies that are deemed critical. The chapter starts by clearing up a fundamental BPI misconception.

Clarifying Business Process Integration

The first point you need to understand about *Business Process Integration* is that it really isn't about integration. Before you completely dismiss this proposition, let me explain what I mean by this. Business processes are logical entities. Although these business processes may map to discrete physical elements, it is generally the exception rather than the rule. When I speak of BPI technology employed to "integrate processes," I am actually referring to the expression, execution, and inspection of a logical workflow. This workflow may involve the integration of data, but it may simply be a series of interconnected tasks that have no implications for data integration whatsoever. On the other hand, Enterprise Application Integration (EAI) technologies operate at a physical level, where messages from a source application are actually transformed and delivered to the target application. Let me put it in another way: BPI is activity-driven, whereas EAI is clearly data-driven.

Perhaps before you understand BPI, you should first understand the essential significance of business processes. Business processes are a series of interconnected business activities. All business activities within a business process are discrete tasks that provide little value to the organization unless they are conducted in sequence and incorporate the right decisions. The fundamental value of the business process is that it provides the protocol that enables business activities to have coherence within the organization and achieve the desired result.

Each business process is made up of a combination of basic business process elements. The four types of business process elements are start events, tasks, decisions, and end events. These are illustrated in Figure 6.1.

Start events trigger the beginning of a business process. A start event may often be an externally initiated event. For instance, a Web-based purchasing transaction process may be set in motion with a start event defined by a prospective customer browsing the online product catalog. For a given business process, usually one or more tasks are defined. In a typical business process, decisions are made along the way. Most commonly, these decision points define a business rule using Boolean logic or a timer as a key enabler. The difference between the two is pretty obvious. A decision point for a purchasing process assessing the following rule— "if customer has made more than three purchases of similar items, inform customer of special product offer"—is an example of using Boolean logic as part of a business rule. However, the decision point—"if no response from customer in 30 seconds, automatically remove special offer"—is a timer-based rule. Finally, some processes may be ended by an external end event. Having such an event is not essential from a practical standpoint because an event could conclude simply when the last task in the business process branch is completed.

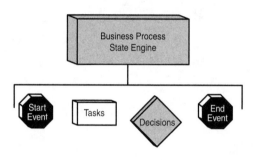

FIGURE 6.1

Business process elements.

In one sense, BPI is far more encompassing than you may have initially perceived. A BPI solution must address the *who*, *what*, and *how* of a business process as indicated in Figure 6.2. Integrating business processes actually implies the synthesis of business protocols, business organizations, and business data.

The definition of an integrated business process must reference *who* participates in the process, either by virtue of direct intervention or by having responsibility for a process segment. BPI solutions should be able to draw on organizational directories and resource databases. This can be accomplished as part of an "import tool" or a programmable API. Addressing the issue of *what* data is affected in the business process is also important. Relevant corporate data will likely be acted on as part of the integrated business process. Interaction with this corporate data may be simplistic and necessitate little more than either reading a record or placing an entry in a database. However, it may be more complex, requiring data to be translated and transformed. These more complex situations call for the invocation of EAI technology, that is, integration brokers. Finally, the BPI solution must address *how* business transactions are conducted. The essence of business process definition entails specifying the protocol and sequence of business activity.

BPI is a vital e-Business Integration technology because it links business activity, data, and resources together under a sequenced activity-driven framework. How does BPI actually work? It can be best unpacked as you examine the primary functional layers of BPI: process modeling, process management, and process analysis.

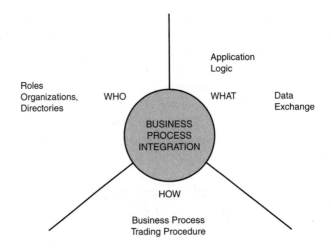

FIGURE 6.2
Understanding Business Process Integration.

Process Modeling

BPI allows the user to semantically represent integration in terms of business process constructs. It means that the flow of corporate information is described in the context and language of business processes, not data. Implementing BPI appropriately begins with process modeling. Process modeling entails the specification of a logical model based on business process interactions. These business process interactions are represented graphically in general workflow syntax. Although there have been discussions promoting the use of the standard Unified Modeling Language (UML) notation, most product offerings have yet to embrace it.

Process models describe the structure and function of the business processes. When I speak of the function of a business process, I refer to work performed by the business process described in terms of business activity. This could be business decisions made or specific business activity, such as the registration of a new customer in a Sales Order process. Business process *structure* refers to the logical flow or progression of the business process. The structure of a business process describes how an individual business activity is linked with another in order to result in a business process. This could constitute decisions, work performed, or synchronization. Modeling at the business process level makes sense because it is intuitively how the business analyst would typically describe the operational flow of activity and information. Figure 6.3 illustrates the business process modeled by a process integration tool.

From this top-tier logical representation of the business process, links may be established to following entities:

- Subprocesses that represent lower-level business activity
- Work forms that require human intervention in the process flow

- Business applications that encapsulate business logic and data
- Custom code that performs discrete processing

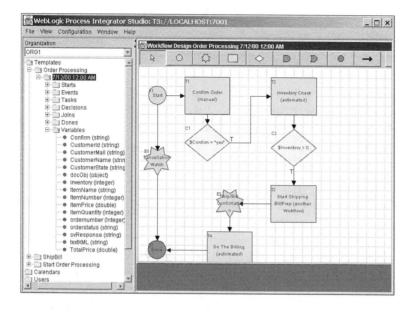

FIGURE 6.3

Business Process Modeling Example—BEA Weblogic Process Integrator.

Process Templates

Some leading experts in the BPI space, such as Brett Adams from Verve Inc., promote the importance of delineating between process definition and process execution. The idea is that the expression of a planned business process should be abstracted from the running systems and managed separately. This is accomplished through the introduction of a process template.

You can think of a process template as a reusable process model. This model is not bound to physical systems and can be managed independently from the runtime process. By treating the design-time template as a separate element, the process designer may actually construct common processes as reusable components. A more complex process may be constructed from individual process templates. Augmenting a running process with a subprocess branch may be as simple as applying a subprocess template. Ultimately, the benefit of a process template is the ability to manage designed processes as reusable components in the same way as code components may be reused.

The introduction of the notion of a business process template may be a good point for me to pause and clarify the terminology used. For the purposes of the discussion in this chapter, I will use the term *process template* to refer to the planned business process defined at design time.

I may also use the term *process template* and *process model* interchangeably. I will generally use the term *business process* to refer to the enacted running business process (that is, Customer Service Complaint process steps through how a customer complaint is handled for resolution). *Business process instance* is a term used to refer to the specific execution of a business process (that is, Customer Complaint processing for customer ID #123-456).

B2B Process Integration

One of the most compelling uses for BPI is not the integration of corporate internal processes but rather the management of B2B processes. Although integrating internal corporate processes drives efficiency and cost savings, the management of B2B processes often drives revenue. These B2B processes govern the protocol of business transactions among partners, suppliers, distributors, and manufacturers.

Managing B2B processes between trading participants over a public network results in a number of additional requirements, not least of which is the introduction of fine-grained control over processes. Processes are defined at design time to be either public or private. Public processes are visible and shared between participants in the trading space. Private processes, on the other hand, are limited in scope to within the enterprise and not known or accessible by external entities. This delineation between public and private processes allows the accessibility to a process to be managed as an attribute of the process. This means by merely setting an attribute, the process can be deemed private or public, hence applicable for internal or B2B process integration.

Practical Limitations

Ultimately, if a BPI "holy grail" exists, it is the idea of being able to define a business process model and have a complete integration implementation automatically generated by the click of a single button. Unfortunately, this doesn't really work in real life. Most BPI products are unable to generate the more complex parts of the integration implementation, such as "application adapter" interactions. The limiting factor is not primarily a technology issue, but one of explicit definition. The logical business process model is simply insufficient in describing the details necessary to build the physical implementation.

However, it doesn't mean that the approach of business process modeling as a precursor to integration work is without merit; just be cautious of empty promises of auto-magically generating integration implementations from a business process model. It also highlights the need for an effective model of how BPI and EAI technologies should work together.

As I mentioned earlier, the traditional EAI approach emphasizes the physical integration framework. With EAI, the construction of an integration flow requires the user to describe the connection in terms of schema mapping and data transformations. Working at the physical data level carries certain advantages when it comes to integration. For one thing, mapping the design phase to the runtime phase is a lot easier when you operate at the physical data level at all times. Herein lies the challenge with BPI: Modeling business processes may be intuitive, but at some point, the process definition stage must lead to implementing integration at the physical layer.

Process Management

You can actually think of business processes as long-running transactions. BPI allows for these transactions to be managed through the BPI runtime engine. Unlike EAI, the BPI runtime does not really move information from point A to point B. Instead, the BPI provides the following process management functionality:

- Process execution
- Process transaction management
- Process monitoring
- Process auditing

Process Execution

Process execution begins with enacting the runtime business process from a planned process template. When enacted, it entails the execution of discrete steps for a business process. The process begins with a start event that serves as an initiating trigger. After the process is triggered, the executing business process begins to perform tasks or units of work. Generally, this work is conducted sequentially although sometimes the business process will engage in two or more parallel branches of work simultaneously. This is known as *process parallelism*. Process parallelism leads to the importance for other supporting functionality, such as synchronization and transaction management.

Synchronization is a process checkpoint to resolve two parallel paths such that path A does not continue until it is resolved with path B. The example in Figure 6.4 illustrates the use of parallelism and synchronization.

Process Transaction Management

Often, these parallel paths must complete work that makes up a part of an overall business transaction. In other words, parallel business processes can be regarded as long-running transactions. Unlike database transactions that are short lived, these long-running transactions can take place over the course of days, weeks, or months. With database and other XA-compliant transactions, the state of the target entities is locked or protected until each subtask is completed successfully. If any task is not completed successfully, the transaction is rolled back, and each entity is restored to its former state. This cannot be done with long-running transactions. Holding the state of an application or process tasks for possibly weeks is unacceptable. The other limitation is that even if it were acceptable to do so, unfortunately, it is often impossible because most applications do not support an XA-compliant transaction interface. This renders it impossible to roll back to a prior state if one of the process branches fails to successfully execute.

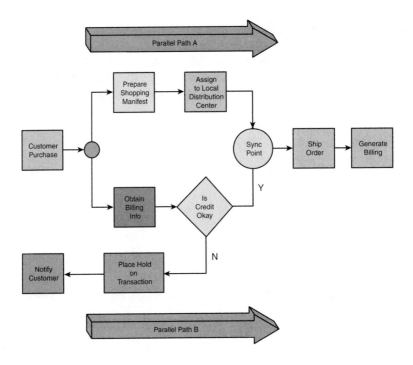

FIGURE 6.4

Parallelism and synchronization in action.

For long-running transactions in which the target systems support transactions, true XA-style transaction management may be possible in theory. However, because that is unlikely, a better technique must be employed. What is commonly used to manage long-running transactions is a technique known as *compensation*. Instead of rolling back to a prior state when tasks fail, compensation allows for execution of a transaction that compensates or corrects the previously committed transaction. Figure 6.5 illustrates how it might be applied in a business process.

In this example, a fast-track interviewing process may complete final checks while preparing the standard new employee setup. In this example, the new employee candidate is engaged with a security-clearance process and employment reference check while new employee setup requests are processed. If the candidate fails to gain the necessary security clearance, other preparatory activities, such as setting up an email account or submitting an entry for a new computer, must be reversed immediately. The compensating transaction in this event may be a process that deletes the new email account and cancels the request for the new computer.

Process Monitoring

Process monitoring is fundamentally about state management of the business process. The BPI engine not only must be able to execute a given step of the process, but also be "aware" of the step progression of any business process instance. Within each BPI engine is a finite state management component. It ensures that the state of each instance of a process in execution is known. This permits the inspection of a business process instance. For example, in an order-fulfillment process, the BPI should be able to address inquiries regarding the step at which a specific customer order is currently being processed.

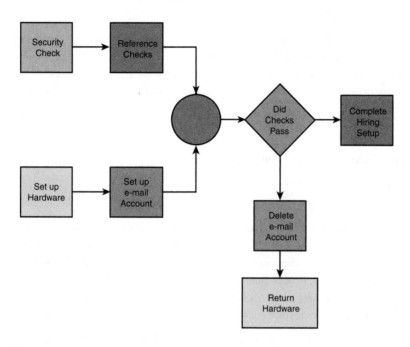

FIGURE 6.5
Snippet of New Employee Hiring Process.

This ability to provide up-to-date information about a business process instance has broad usage for supply chain management, customer relationship management, and just-in-time manufacturing.

Process Auditing

Process auditing leads to the ability to perform process analysis. Information regarding each process activity is logged in to a database or process metric warehouse. Among the key elements logged include the following:

- Time stamp of process instance activity beginning
- Time stamp of process instance activity completing
- Specific error or warning codes
- Performance statistics
- Acknowledgment for successful outcomes

Most BPI engines provide an audit API such that participating applications that perform work may also provide fine-grained metrics on work completed that is typically embedded within the application.

Process Analysis

Process analysis is conducted to link process statistics to business metrics. The historical data collected is used to analyze the process efficiency and execution path. The process analysis phase is post process; that is, it is conducted after the process has been executed over a period of time. The process metrics can be used to answer questions such as the following:

- What is the average time required to complete a business process for a given span of time?
- What is the critical path in a process?
- How do you detect process bottlenecks?
- How many times was a particular decision made?
- How can the process be optimized?

To answer these and other questions, the process analysis must be able to act on both instance data as well as aggregated data. The process metric warehouse must provide access to individual instances of a process. As an example, every metric related to process ID #123 is logged to the process metric database. Process analysis also requires processing historical data in an aggregated fashion. For example, metrics for the customer order fulfillment process are averaged or "rolled up" in some manner such that statistics per process may be assessed.

So far, you've learned what the BPI system does in terms of primary functional layers—modeling, management, and analysis. Now, look at how the BPI system functions as a running system. The BPI system should be viewed in terms of design-time and runtime components. In Figure 6.6 shows how the design-time system works.

As you can see in Figure 6.6, the user models the business process at design time, resulting in process models or templates. Many BPI design-time tools can work in a disconnected mode. When used in this way, the modeling tool stores a copy of a business process in the tool's local repository. This copy of the process template is actually checked out of the central BPI system repository. It is locked by the user and not available for edits by anyone else. When modifications to the local process flow copy are completed, it is unlocked and checked back into the central BPI system repository.

At runtime, a component of the BPI engine called the *executor* loads and enacts the business process model, resulting in a running business process. This is illustrated in Figure 6.7. The finite state management component monitors the state of each instance of the enacted process. For example, with the Customer Service Complaint process, it can independently track each specific customer complaint currently being processed. The state management component also maintains global data that is acted on by the process elements. As the business process executes, it needs to invoke business logic entities such as applications or components to perform a measure of work.

At times, these entities need to reference data provided by a prior executing component or store data so that it might be used by a component in a forthcoming step in the process. For instance, in a customer order scenario, the sales tax may be calculated during an initial customer purchase phase and still be required in a later stage for registering sales tax with Accounting. Also shown in Figure 6.7 are the audit component and dispatcher. The audit component is responsible for logging the process metrics to a persistent storage. The dispatcher plays a critical role by initiating work either in terms of running an EJB component or executing work list items.

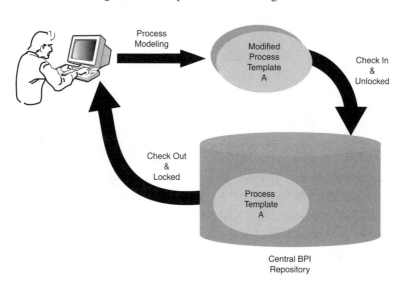

FIGURE 6.6

The Business Process Integration Design Time.

The entire BPI system has to be centrally manageable. This means a couple of different things. First, it entails having the ability to control process elements. This means such simple tasks as starting, stopping, or suspending execution business process elements. For instance, if a process is currently at a decision point requiring human intervention, you may choose to suspend the process at that point until necessary data is available for the human participant to make the appropriate decision.

It also means support for SNMP management frameworks such as IBM Tivoli and CA Unicenter. In addition to simply providing systems management, these SNMP management frameworks can be used in the context of managing business processes. Critical systems resource conditions such as application availability or business resource conditions such as abnormal backlogged orders in a queue may be flagged to the appropriate individuals by firing what is known as an *SNMP trap*. It is an SNMP-based alerting mechanism that is recognized by all systems management frameworks, including the aforementioned Unicenter and Tivoli.

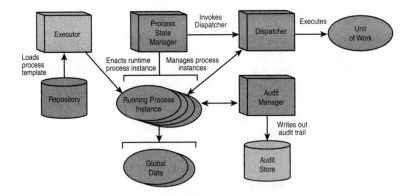

FIGURE 6.7
The Business Process Integration Run Time.

Leading Business Process Integration Products

I've chosen to highlight three primary products in this section. Each is somewhat different, but all three have compelling BPI technology to consider. The chosen BPI products are from the following vendors:

- BEA Systems (WebLogic Process Integrator)
- Extricity (Alliance Manager)
- Versata (Verve Workflow Engine)

I will provide a general commentary on each to facilitate your understanding of each offering. If you are in the process of selecting a product in this category, you might use this information as a *starting* point for evaluating the technology.

Alliance Manager (Extricity)

Extricity, more than any other company, understood early on that B2Bi and BPI are inextricably linked. It staked its claim as a pioneer by focusing the process integration not on integration of internally focused processes, but on B2B process integration. In my mind, this is most clearly evident by its support of XML and its implementation of process management.

Extricity's flagship product is the B2B Alliance Manager, which allows the user to do the following:

- Manage partner collaborations
- Model processes
- Execute processes
- Control processes
- Manage the physical environment

The Alliance Manager is composed of three primary components:

- **Process Manager** allows for the fine-grained control and management of the process. One aspect of process management that is characteristically an Extricity innovation is the delineation of each process either as private or public. Since Extricity introduced this concept, other vendors have followed suit, but Extricity has implemented it as a core element of the Process Manager.

- **Channel Manager** provides the ability to coordinate collaborations between partners. It allows the user to define communication mechanisms used in collaborations. It also adheres to XML-based standards such as RosettaNet as well as older EDI formats.

- **Adapter Manager** handles connectivity and access to legacy and packaged applications. A design-time component known as the Adapter Designer and a runtime component known as the Adapter Server are also available.

WebLogic Process Integrator (BEA Systems)

With version 1.0 released late in the third quarter of 2000, BEA System's WebLogic Process Integrator (WLPI) is the newest entrant in this space. However, it is not a brand new product but simply the first release under the BEA label. WLPI was originally JFlow, a leading workflow product. BEA acquired the technology when it acquired the Workflow Automation Corporation, the company that built JFlow. Immediately, JFlow was recrafted around the J2EE platform and many of its services rewritten as EJB components. The adherence to the EJB component model and its strong support for standards such as the J2EE and XML is, in fact, one of WLPI's primary distinctions.

WLPI is a client/server-based workflow management system. It is built on the WebLogic Server (WLS) infrastructure, and installing WLS is a prerequisite to running WLPI. It also requires a database as a persistence engine. WLPI version 1.0 requires Oracle; later point versions support MS SQL Server.

The central component of WLPI is the runtime process engine, which is responsible for initiating workflows, monitoring workflow instances, and facilitating control over a running workflow. The WLPI process engine, during the course of task execution, may interact with other systems in three ways. First, it may receive and submit application events in the form of XML documents or JMS messages. Second, as part of executing a workflow task, the process engine can also invoke an EJB component to perform a measure of work. Finally, it can simply perform a command-line `exec` on any executable file.

The primary WLPI user tool is the WebLogic Process Integration Studio. Through this GUI tool, the user can design workflow templates; perform data administration tasks such as assigning users, roles, and business operations; and monitor workflow instances.

Verve Component Workflow (Versata)

Verve, recently acquired by Versata, takes a completely different approach from most vendors. The Verve Component Workflow product is unique in that it was designed from the ground up to be an embeddable component. In this light, process integration is regarded as functionality first rather than a strategic end-user product. This strategic difference is reflected completely in the way the product is constructed, packaged, and sold, but most of all in the way it was defined from the beginning.

In the Verve Component Workflow—Concepts document, Verve Component Workflow is defined as "a toolset for the proactive analysis, compression, automation, inspection, and integration of business processes."

The primary runtime component of the Verve Component Workflow product is the Verve process server, which is based on CORBA and is composed of a set of subservices. These subservices handle capabilities such as persistence, administration, and audit.

Because Verve Workflow is meant to be used as an embeddable component, exploring the APIs that allow a user to leverage Verve's functional capability may be valuable. The Verve Workflow product provides three primary types of APIs: Client APIs, Integration APIs, and Extension APIs. The Client APIs provide interfaces to initiate the process and manipulate the worklists. The Integration APIs allow the user to manage organizations and audit the workflow. Finally, the examples of the Extension APIs include APIs for persistence and invocation.

In my evaluation of Verve, I believe the product to be rich in functionality and well designed from the perspective of interoperability. Its approach makes it compelling when considering process integration as a functional element of a larger solution.

Summary

As you learned at the beginning of this chapter, BPI is not about integration but about managing the state. Business processes are, in a sense, long-running business transactions, and BPI is about being able to monitor the progress of a process instance. BPI can be defined by three primary facets: process modeling, process management, and process analysis. Each facet was covered in detail in this chapter, providing you with an understanding of the functional elements of process integration.

The next chapter will discuss XML. It is difficult to delve into any technology arena without seeing how it is affected by XML. The use of XML and how it fits in the e-Business Integration framework is the basis of Chapter 7, "XML Standards and Integration," which will provide an overview of XML, discuss the significance of XML in integration, and examine new developments in XML standards.

XML Standards and Integration

"The more they overthink the plumbing, the easier it is to stop up the drain."
—Scotty in Star Trek III: The Search for Spock

IN THIS CHAPTER

Because of developments in the past couple of years, it seems implausible to mention e-Business without a discussion about the impact of the eXtensible Markup Language (XML). XML has particularly been linked to B2B, but its impact extends well beyond that single domain. Its influence has seemingly permeated every technology area, ranging from enabling online business transactions to creating new scripting languages.

This chapter and the next will explore how XML is leveraged for e-Business Integration. However, to explore it effectively, you must first understand the relevant XML standards that pertain to integration. This chapter provides much of the necessary technical overview for understanding these technologies. The following chapter will cover how these technologies are leveraged and applied in solving the e-Business Integration problem.

The Emergence of XML

The eXtensible Markup Language (XML) is one of the most significant technologies to emerge in recent years, quickly gathering industrywide momentum. XML's roots can be traced back to the Standard Generalized Markup Language (SGML). SGML is a flexible language used to mark up or describe data. Used widely in the document publishing industry, SGML was noted for its power and complexity. XML emerged as a simpler SGML—all the power of SGML without the complexity associated with using it. In fact, XML is actually a subset of SGML, maintaining most of the SGML syntax and rules.

Because the application of SGML gave rise to the Hypertext Markup Language (HTML), perhaps it comes as no surprise that XML was initially positioned as simply an improved HTML. Since those early days, XML has emerged to become the *de facto* standard for data exchange. Yet, XML is far more than either of those descriptions might imply. XML is a meta-markup language, providing a flexible way to describe the structure and content of a document. Being a markup language means that XML enables you to create tags that carry specialized meaning that may be applied to describe the content and structure of a document. Unlike HTML, where the markup tags are predefined, through XML you can derive other markup languages that describe data suited for specific industry domains. For instance, a data exchange format for describing financial transaction data called Open Financial Exchange (OFX) is inherently XML-based. OFX is an example of what is known as an *XML vocabulary*—that is, an XML-based markup language for describing industry or application-specific data formats. Other examples of XML vocabularies include the Chemical Markup Language (CML) and Wireless Markup Language (WML).

Perhaps what makes XML so compelling is the fact that it is not simply technology but a standard. Since 1994, the XML standard has been defined and governed by the World Wide Web Consortium (W3C). If you want to learn more about the W3C and XML, you can begin by visiting the W3C Web site at www.w3c.org.

Why the Hype over XML?

Why has XML been so significant and widely adopted by the technical community? To appreciate the impact of XML, you need to understand the benefits that XML brings to the party. Five primary strengths of XML have led to the widespread acceptance of this exciting technology:

1. **Powerful meta language**—XML provides an easily used mechanism by which other markup languages can be developed for specific needs or business domains. This is evidenced by the proliferation of markup languages such as the Chemical Markup Language (CML), Voice Markup Language (VoxML), and Vector Markup Language (VML).

2. **Human readable**—XML is generally easily understood because its text-based form lends to readability. When you look at an XML document, you can generally understand the structure and data contained within the document.

3. **Common open standard**—XML is not proprietary; it is not tied to a specific proprietary browser, editor, or interpreter. Instead, XML is a computing industry standard that has found broad acceptance. As a result, it can be applied and evolved according to the needs of the industry as a whole.

4. **Separation of content and presentation format**—XML cleanly delineates between the semantic content of the document and the presentation of the document. Unlike HTML, which encapsulates both the presentation and semantic content of the document, XML provides a separation of both elements.

5. **Platform independent**—Many people refer to XML as "portable data." It is both platform and language independent, which permits for its application in a heterogeneous enterprise environment. You could use XML in a C++ application on Windows 2000 as easily as with a Java application running on Linux.

You'll learn more details about these and other benefits of XML later, especially as it applies in the area of e-Business Integration, but this discussion will do for now. Suffice it to say, with the kind of hype that has preceded this technology, there are limitations that govern its use in integration, and they will be discussed in due course as well. Now, it's time to actually discuss what the XML standard is all about.

The XML Standard

XML is not simply a single standard but, in fact, a set of technology standards that define various aspects defining, manipulating, displaying, and managing data. When you hear about XML, what is often referred to is the XML 1.0 base specification. The base specification defines the syntax and rules defining the legitimacy of an XML document. XML processors enforce these rules during the parsing of the document.

However, beyond that base specification, there are several other specifications. In particular, you will learn about the following in this and the next chapter:

- **XML Schema**—An XML standard for defining document templates that describe the structure of an XML document. It replaces the use of Document Type Definitions (DTDs).
- **DOM**—The Document Object Model is an object-styled mechanism to access and manipulate XML documents.
- **SAX**—Although DOM is an effective means for XML document access, the Simple API for XML (SAX) is an alternative and newer way to do so, addressing the capability to receive events.
- **XSLT**—This is an extension of the Extensible Stylesheet Language (XSL) specification specifically to address the need to transform XML documents to and from any other text-based documents. The following chapter specifically addresses the use of XML for e-Business Integration scenarios.

Before looking at each of the preceding standards, you need to first understand the basics of what constitutes an XML document.

What Exactly Is XML?

As mentioned previously, XML documents are text-based, although not all text documents are XML. For a text document to be "truly XML," it has to conform to rules of structure and grammar defined in the XML 1.0 base specification. This is what is known as a "well-formed" XML document. An XML processor is a software program that parses an XML document and checks for compliance of a well-formed document based on a set of rules.

The primary grammatical rules that define a well-formed XML document are described in the following sections. These sections also draw attention to aspects of XML that are related to but not explicitly stated as rules.

Element Names Must Conform to XML Conventions

XML is not particularly restrictive when it comes to naming conventions; however, you must adhere to some general naming rules:

- Names cannot begin with numbers or special punctuation characters.
- Names cannot contain spaces.
- Names cannot begin with xml as the prefix.
- The colon (:) character is reserved by the XML specification and should not be used.

I've excluded a couple more rules, but the preceding cover the main points of the XML naming conventions.

Start Tag Must Have a Corresponding End Tag

A fundamental difference between XML and SGML is that a start tag must have a corresponding end tag. In SGML, not every element requires a matching start and end tag. This, in turn, makes parsing the SGML document particularly tricky. Not so with XML. Every start tag needs to have a matching end tag. The code segment in Listing 7.1 is an example of a Hello World XML document with matching tags.

LISTING 7.1   A Well-Formed Hello Word XML Document

```
<? xml version = '1.0' encoding = 'UTF-8' standalone = 'yes'?>
<MYDOC>
     <GREETING>
          Hello Cruel World
     </GREETING>
</MYDOC>
```

Believe it or not, Listing 7.1 is a complete, well-formed XML document. The XML document is based on tags, or markups, that describe the contents of the document. But even in this example, you can see how easy and intuitive the XML syntax really is.

Another point regarding the use of tags is that they can be nested but cannot overlap. This means that "tag pairs" are embedded within other "tags pairs," but the use of these matching tags should not allow for these tag pairs to overlap each other.

Tags Are Case Sensitive

Because tags are case sensitive, you can include a `<GREETING>` tag and `<greeting>` tag within the same document as two separate, unique tags. Doing so can, of course, cause undue confusion. In general, applying case sensitivity to differentiate two unique tags is not a good idea.

If Included, the XML Declaration Should Begin the Document

In the Hello World XML document in Listing 7.1, the tag `<? xml version = '1.0' encoding = 'UTF-16' standalone = 'yes'?>` is referred to as the *XML declaration*. Strictly speaking, having an XML declaration is not a requirement. However, if the declaration is included, it must be at the absolute beginning of the document.

Now take a closer look at the declaration and see what you can learn from it. The `version`, `encoding`, and `standalone` portions of the declaration are called *attributes* of the XML document. The first portion of the XML declaration is fairly self-explanatory. It specifies the version of the XML specification that the document complies with. The second part of the declaration defines the character encoding scheme. In this example, the Unicode encoding scheme is specified by the UTF-16 attribute. Finally, the standalone attribute refers to the fact that this XML document does not depend on other XML documents.

For the record, attributes are not only associated with the XML declaration, but are also name-value pairs that can be placed with any tag. Because I had an opportunity to point this out in the declaration example, I decided to highlight the use of attributes here.

XML Document Should Contain Only One Root Element

A well-formed XML document must contain only one root element that may, in turn, contain other elements. The Hello World example earlier is well formed because the <MYDOC> tag provided the root element, but the example in Listing 7.2 is another attempt at a Hello World document. However, this one is not well formed because the two <GREETING> tags are positioned at the root level.

Listing 7.2   A Poorly Formed XML Document That Has Multiple Root Elements

```
<? xml version = "1.0">
<GREETING>
    Hello My World
</GREETING>
 <GREETING>
    Hello Cruel World
</GREETING>
```

This listing leads to the following insight regarding XML documents: XML documents are organized hierarchically. If you examine the structure of an XML document, you will discover that it can be viewed as a hierarchical tree with branches and leaves. In fact, this is a common way to view and reference an XML document and the elements contained within. Figure 7.1 shows this hierarchical tree view of an XML document for a customer address.

The tree representation of the Customer document begins at the root with Customer. The next level contains the Name, Address, and AccountID. Finally, the last level provides the elements for defining the Name and Address items specifically. Each data item on the tree is commonly referred to as an *element*. When an element contains other elements, it is said to be the *parent* element, whereas the lower-level elements are known as *child* elements.

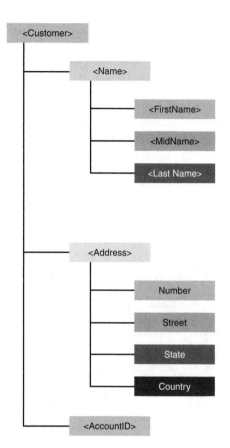

FIGURE 7.1

XML tree view.

XML Validity—Beyond Well-Formed Documents

The well-formed characteristic of an XML document speaks to the compliance of its *physical attributes* to the XML specification. The validity of the XML document addresses its conformity to the constraints of its *logical definition*. The well-formed characteristic takes precedence because a valid document is always well formed, but a well-formed document is not necessarily valid.

An XML document is considered valid if its syntax is successfully checked for compliance. For a document to be checked for validity by the XML processor, it has to include the `<!DOCTYPE>` tag. This tag is known as a *document type declaration* (never refer to it as the DTD; that's reserved for the *Document Type Definition*). It references the specific DTD associated with the XML document. A series of document types may be defined for a specific vertical industry or application. When grouped together in this fashion, it is sometimes referred to as an *XML-defined vocabulary*. These XML vocabularies are specified by a series of DTDs.

The DTD is a simplified holdover from the SGML heritage. It provides a means for defining an XML vocabulary and is used to validate the logical syntax of the document. A program known as a *validating parser* ensures that a document is not simply well formed but that the syntax applied within the document is in compliance with the definition laid out in the DTD. In this way, the validity of the XML content is ensured.

The DTD can be viewed as control meta data for the XML document. It provides information to describe the constraints for the XML content. Instead of being defined for each and every XML document, a common DTD defining a specific type can be shared by numerous documents, as shown in Figure 7.2.

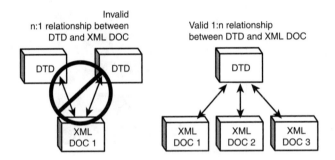

FIGURE 7.2
DTD to XML Relationship and Cardinality.

This "sharing of a common DTD" is particularly useful in B2B data exchanges in which multiple partners can exchange documents with each other based on a common set of DTDs. However, as Figure 7.2 also illustrates, each XML document may only have one DTD.

When a DTD is contained completely within an XML document, it is known as an *internal subset*. It may also exist as an *external subset*, completely outside the XML document in a separate file. Often when you hear about DTDs, the external subset approach is referred to. It might be interesting to take a look at a DTD example. An example of a rather simple DTD is shown in Listing 7.3.

LISTING 7.3   DTD Listing

```
<!DOCTYPE DOCUMENT [
<!ELEMENT CUSTOMER (NAME, ADDRESS)>
<!ELEMENT NAME (FIRSTNAME, MIDNAME, LASTNAME)>
```

LISTING 7.3 Continued

```
<!ELEMENT FIRSTNAME (#PCDATA)>
<!ELEMENT MIDNAME (#PCDATA)>
<!ELEMENT LASTNAME (#PCDATA)>
<!ELEMENT ADDRESS (NUMBER, STREET, STATE)>
<!ELEMENT NUMBER (#PCDATA)>
<!ELEMENT STREET (#PCDATA)>
<!ELEMENT STATE (#PCDATA)>
]>
```

If you're observant, you'll notice something strange right away. That's right—for all the emphasis on XML, it appears that the DTD itself is not XML-compliant. DTDs have the advantage of being able to leverage existing SGML tools. However, the fact that the DTD isn't XML-based raises a number of interesting points of limitation:

1. The DTD is not nearly as easy to follow and read as an XML document. Putting it together can be tedious work.

2. A DTD is not extensible in the way an XML document is. It doesn't provide the capability to aggregate or inherit from other DTDs. For instance, you cannot have a DTD composed and aggregated from other "sub-DTD" documents.

3. Because the DTD isn't XML, you don't have the benefit of using XML tools developed to edit, parse, and validate XML documents.

4. The DTD has poor support for data typing, which simply means that it supports only text strings. There are no specialized definitions for complex types such as date, time, and currency.

The preceding are simply some of the limitations that have led to the development of an XML-based alternative to the DTD.

Enter XML Schemas

As noted previously, DTDs suffer from a number of limitations, most of which stem from its non-XML approach. Recently, XML Schemas have emerged to address some of the most profound weaknesses of the DTD approach. XML Schemas provide the following benefits:

- XML extensibility
- New and improved data typing
- Leveraged XML access and reference mechanisms
- Dynamic schema management

XML Extensibility

XML Schemas allow you to aggregate a master schema document from multiple schemas. They possess the fundamental object-oriented capability for aggregation and inheritance from base schemas. This promotes reuse of schemas and reduces the probability for data management errors.

New and Improved Data Typing

For where XML is going and the myriad ways it is leveraged into various applications, the DTD string typing is insufficient. XML Schemas provide data typing for numeric, date, time, and currency types. They also allow for rich user-defined types.

Leveraged XML Access and Reference Mechanisms

By virtue of being XML-based, schemas can be accessed and traversed using conventional XML-based mechanisms such as DOM. Portions of the schema can be queried and referenced using XPath. The availability of these mechanisms and supporting tools lend to your ability to manage the schemas at a global enterprise level.

Dynamic Schema Management

Your ability to dynamically change the schema is an additional benefit of XML Schemas. It has particular significance in B2B integration scenarios. You'll look into this aspect of XML Schemas when learning about leveraging XML in the next chapter.

XML Schemas at Work

You can understand XML Schemas in a broad sense by grasping three concepts: data types, structures, and the <schema> element. Data types are the basic elements of the XML Schema definition. Data types within XML Schema can be primitive data types, complex derived data types, or user-derived data types. Primitive data types cannot be defined in terms of any other data types. Complex derived data types are specified and built into the XML Schema specification but are derived from other existing types. User-derived types are defined by the user, derived from pre-existing types as well and not built into the specification.

Structures are means for describing a document type. Without getting into the details of structures, suffice it to say that structure declarations allow you to define data types, attributes, and content models in much the same way DTDs do, but you reap the associated benefits of their being XML-based.

Finally, the `<schema>` element is the means by which an XML Schema is associated with an XML document. Attributes of the schema, such as a namespace reference to an XML vocabulary, are declared within the `<schema>` element.

The following XML Schema-based tools are worth mentioning as a point of reference:

- IBM has produced an XML parser, XML4J, that uses schemas to validate an XML document.
- The Xerces parser can be downloaded from the Apache site and has support for schemas.
- XML Authority is an XML schema design tool from Extensibility.

More tools will obviously emerge as schemas become prominent in defining XML documents and replace the use of DTDs.

Accessing and Traversing XML Documents with DOM

XML documents provide a powerful and portable means for describing, containing, and transporting data for e-Business Integration. However, their usefulness is limited unless that data can be easily accessed. That is why it is important that you understand how XML data is stored and defined, to study how that data is accessed and manipulated. DOM and SAX are the two primary mechanisms covered in the rest of this chapter.

Although XML data is stored in a hierarchical fashion, it is often easier to understand the XML document in terms of a tree structure, as shown in Figure 7.3. As such, elements within the XML documents can be viewed as objects. The object model corresponds nicely to the parent-child description of the element relationships at differing levels.

DOM provides two primary capabilities. First, it enables the programmer to build a DOM tree that provides an object model for the XML content. A node in the DOM tree may be a document, notation, entity, element, or even processing instruction. Second, DOM provides generic interfaces for manipulating the object model presented in Figure 7.3. The primary interface for DOM is the Node interface, which has properties that provide information on a particular node or element. It also is composed of methods to navigate the tree, adding, removing, and replacing nodes.

With DOM, a node tree is constructed in memory, and an application can manipulate the document via the object model. This approach is shown in Figure 7.4, where an application first calls the parser. The XML-DOM parser builds the node tree in memory. The application implements the DOM object interfaces to traverse and manipulate the data.

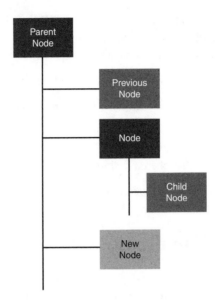

FIGURE 7.3
Node Relationships.

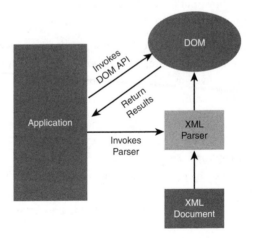

FIGURE 7.4
DOM approach.

DOM is useful when you need to have full navigation of the tree, but depending on what the application needs to do, using DOM may be less than ideal. I'll discuss one of these scenarios next.

The SAX Appeal

Imagine that you have a simple application responsible for receiving purchase requests for office supplies as an XML document via email and checking to ensure that the items are on an approved office supplies list. In this example, the application does not need to have full access to the document or perform any complex manipulations on a node tree. You just want the application to have access to the items on the purchase requisition form in order to approve and route the document appropriately. In fact, as you can see in Figure 7.5, it would be great if the application is notified when the parser detects these data items.

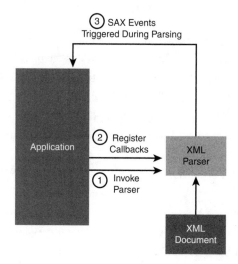

FIGURE 7.5

SAX at work.

Contrast Figure 7.5 with the DOM approach featured in Figure 7.4, and you'll begin to see that, at times with DOM, building an entire tree to traverse seems needlessly redundant, especially when you really need an event-based mechanism to be invoked. That is one of the primary reasons SAX was developed as an alternative way to access XML data.

SAX provides the capability for event notifications by using callbacks. You can use SAX in your application by implementing a SAX parser object, derived from the Xerces SAX parser class from Apache. You can then register one or more of the SAX event-handling interfaces. The primary SAX interfaces are as follows:

- **ContentHandler**—Handles elements and processes instructions and other content items
- **ErrorHandler**—Simply handles errors that occur during the course of parsing
- **EntityResolver**—Handles events for external entities

Each interface has callback methods that are automatically registered by default when the interface is implemented. Keep in mind that SAX is an acronym for Simple API for XML. Part of the appeal of SAX is also its simplicity in implementation.

You may also be surprised to discover that SAX is not a consortium-managed standard but rather stems from the initiative of David Meggison, who is a developer in search of a better way. Since the beginning, he has overseen and directed the development of SAX. If you're interested in finding out more details about SAX, you can visit his Web site at
`http://www.megginson.com/SAX`.

Summary

If you weren't knowledgeable about XML before reading this chapter, you should be well past that obstacle at this point—which is really the intent of this chapter. Besides providing information about the history and significance of XML, this chapter also covered four primary areas of essential XML knowledge, including the following:

- The basics of an XML document as specified in the XML base specification. The chapter discussed what constitutes a well-formed and valid XML document. It also covered DTDs and its limitations.

- The emergence and use of XML Schema. Specific benefits of XML Schema over DTDs were discussed.

- The representation of an XML document as a hierarchical object model. The chapter discussed how to use DOM to traverse and manipulate an XML document.

- A brief discussion of SAX as an alternative, event-based mechanism for accessing and filtering XML data.

Unlike most of the other technologies covered in previous chapters, XML is not a technology product, but rather a set of standards that can be applied in numerous ways, including integration. With a firm grasp on the XML technology, you're ready to move on to the next chapter and look at how XML is leveraged in e-Business Integration.

Leveraging XML for Integration

"Technological progress is like an axe in the hands of a pathological criminal."
—Albert Einstein

IN THIS CHAPTER

In the preceding chapter, I discussed XML in very general terms without providing a context for how it affects e-Business Integration. I did so deliberately to provide a foundation for XML, setting the stage for discussions in this chapter. The fact is that integration is profoundly affected by the use of XML, and in this chapter, I will discuss how XML is leveraged for integration. This chapter delves into the discussion of XML with an integration-centric view. It also explores extensions of XML into the realm of data transformation, databases, and distributed computing. With increasing attention given to B2B exchanges, this chapter also examines the work around RosettaNet, the leading consortium for B2B trading standards.

The Dawning of XML-Centric Integration

The idea of XML applied for integration wouldn't be considered surprising or groundbreaking in any way. After all, isn't much of integration about the exchange of information? As information becomes packaged as XML documents, isn't integrating with XML a given? Certainly, the exchange of XML documents is nothing new. However, with regard to XML-centric integration, you can think of the former as simply the toddler stage of progressive development.

The use of XML as a basic framework for integration is immature, but it is inevitable for two reasons:

- The emergence of networked B2B communities
- The need for enterprise transparency

Networked B2B Communities

As B2B trading exchanges create an open forum for trading, what naturally emerges is a global network of trading communities that are linked together. This happens because companies will participate in multiple communities, depending on the role they play in the supply chain. For example, ACME Manufacturing may participate in a B2B exchange as a purchaser of raw materials but be a component supplier in another B2B community.

Trading demands will fuel the growth of networked trading communities because price and availability of goods continue to be the primary metrics for buying. In simple terms, this means if ACME Manufacturing cannot get raw materials at one exchange for the right price, they will shop somewhere else.

The Need for Enterprise Transparency

The need for enterprise transparency is just a fancy way of saying that the integration of applications within the enterprise must be viewed as simply an element of the total e-Business Integration picture. There is a growing need for companies to provide corporate application data as part of the supply chain. EAI is typically focused on intra-enterprise application integration, but the need for the enterprise to be transparent will grow. Allowing customers, partners, and suppliers to directly interact with enterprise application data is inevitable. It's really the reason that I've referred to e-Business Integration rather than EAI. It isn't that EAI is going away; actually, it's just changing.

What Is XML-Centric Integration?

XML-Centric Integration means more than simply packaging data as XML documents. It actually means providing a framework for integration based on key XML technologies. Let's examine how XML is applied today in a corporate enterprise. Figure 8.1 provides a typical conceptual architectural view of information exchange today.

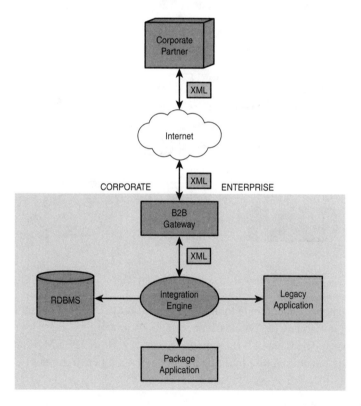

FIGURE 8.1

Leveraging XML for the Corporate Enterprise.

You'll find that XML is prominently featured in an external focused manner. It is the *lingua franca* when participating in B2B transactions. Documents or data exposed to the outside world are often conducted in XML, but within the n-tier enterprise environment, XML is used sparingly. At times, a common expression of data may be converted to XML mostly to interface with the few applications that have a rich XML interface.

Taking a closer look at the way XML is used within the enterprise and with enterprise applications in Figure 8.2 reveals that ample opportunity exists for XML to be leveraged in an n-tier distributed computing environment.

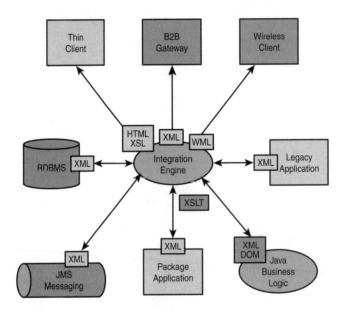

FIGURE 8.2

XML in a Distributed Environment.

The elements of integration continue to apply. The need for extracting and interfacing with applications does not go away. Complex transformations, routing, business logic components, and meta-data management are still relevant and necessary. However, XML can be applied to radically affect the integration of a traditional n-tier computing environment by providing the following:

- Enterprise object-relational model
- XML-based data transformation
- XML-based distributed computing model
- XML-based meta data

Enterprise Object-Relational Model: XML and Databases

In the distributed enterprise architecture, you'll find the layers of presentation, application logic, and databases. Increasingly, the presentation layer is a thin client and XML-based. The application logic is typically encapsulated in business components that reside in a mid-level tier. The database is a relational database. A dichotomy exists between the relational data model and business component model. The relational data is generally accessed as a two-dimensional recordset of rows and columns, whereas the business component model is object-oriented. This has led to a new kind of component known as a *data object* in which the resultset of the database query is not contained within a recordset structure but rather within a data object. The Advanced Data Object (ADO) provided by Microsoft is an example of how a data object works. This requires object-to-relational (O-R) mapping, as shown in Figure 8.3.

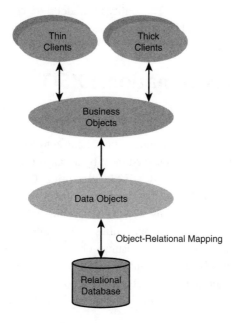

FIGURE 8.3

Data Objects providing O-R mapping.

How does this affect the crafting of an integration solution? Often, to address the movement of data between applications, data must be represented as objects to interact with integration components responsible for transformation, routing, and filtering. This can mean that the integration components will contain custom code to process the data as a two-dimensional recordset. This is not very intuitive and can be cumbersome. Using data objects like ADO would be a fine approach, except that ADO works only on the Windows environment, and you will likely end up with multiple data objects, each providing the O-R mapping needed for each primary database.

XML can play a significant role here. As you learned in the preceding chapter, the XML document model can be viewed as a hierarchical tree with node elements functioning as objects. DOM, in fact, provides a model with interfaces, allowing the programmer to manipulate the document as objects.

This is powerful stuff. Instead of proprietary and platform-specific data objects like ADO, XML-DOM can provide a portable and dynamic data object model.

Modeling relational data with XML establishes the O-R mapping between two-dimensional recordsets and the DOM object model. Columns in the resultset usually map to elements within the XML document. In the case of a simple single-table query, the root element is often used to represent the named table. With the advent of XML Schemas, one of the hurdles of using XML for this purpose is averted. The ability to model the rich typing in databases is addressed. Previously, the use of DTDs proved inadequate in expressing richer data types such as integers, floats, date, and time.

XML-Based Transformations: XSLT

I could just as easily have covered XSLT as part of the preceding chapter. After all, XSLT is used extensively primarily to convert XML to HTML for presentation purposes. However, because XSLT has special significance to integration, I chose to defer its discussion until this chapter. In particular, a B2B scenario is served most by a transformation technology like XSLT. If Corporation ABC wants to trade with ACME Manufacturing, the use of common representations for business objects such as Invoice or Customer Order is vitally important. Complicating the matter is the reality that each company will likely have proprietary business objects defined based on internal business processes and applications. For seamless interchange, both companies could choose to adopt a set of common business object definitions. This approach unfortunately will ripple changes through each organization's business processes. Preferably, they could choose to retain their own internal business object definitions and use XSLT to perform dynamic transformations between the two companies. This process is shown in Figure 8.4.

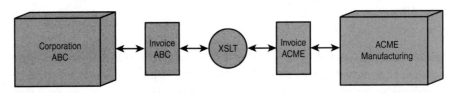

FIGURE 8.4

XSLT providing transformation between two entities.

What is XSLT? XSLT is a specialized language for performing transformations patterned after the broader eXtensible Stylesheet Language (XSL). XSL is made up of two basic Stylesheet processing language elements: XSL Formatting Objects and XSLT. Because XSL Formatting Objects are extremely new, most XSL processor engines perform XSLT processing.

Figure 8.5 illustrates the basic operation of an XSLT transformation. The source XML document is transformed by the XSLT processor based on the supplied XSLT style sheet.

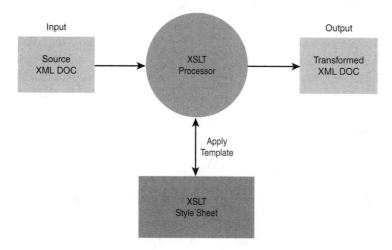

FIGURE 8.5
Basic Operation of XSLT.

A fundamental aspect of the XSLT style sheet is something known as a *template*, which is defined by the `<xsl:template>` element. A template consists of a match attribute and the contents of the template. The match attribute allows the XSLT engine to scan the document for a match on a specified element. For instance, two companies want to exchange invoice documents but discover that Company A uses a six-letter invoice number, whereas Company B uses a nine-letter invoice number with a three-letter prefix. An XSLT engine could seek to resolve this difference between the two invoice documents by finding the invoice number element and appending a designated prefix for output based on a style-sheet matching attribute.

With XSLT, the transformation is defined by declaring the output structure described in the style sheet. It's important to note that the style sheet does not provide instructions for processing transformations but rather defines a deterministic result. This is a powerful approach, but will XSLT suffice as an all-purpose transformation mechanism? I don't think it's ready for all types of transformation just yet. The three limitations described in the following three sections seem apparent at this point.

Text-Based Transformation Only

XSLT is appropriate for transformation of XML and text-based documents but it cannot transform data that comes from richer data sources with nontext data. This especially limits its use in an internal EAI integration scenario where transformation of application data may include varied data types such as floats or doubles.

Many-to-Many Transformations

XSLT is suited for B2B transformations because most B2B transactions can be reduced to interactions between two parties; not so with EAI type transformations, which can involve many parties with complex relationships. For instance, you may receive input messages from two source applications, both supplying a customer address. You can compare both addresses to determine which address is more recent. Then you can create a new message based on the newer address and cross-referenced product item information to send to the distribution center as a shipping manifest. You also can send a notification email to the sales manager, appending the projected ship date. This many-to-many imperative style transformation is not the kind that XSLT is easily used for.

Pattern-Matching Style Transformation Is Limited

XSLT is based on seeking a match and declaring a defined output based on the template. However, not all transformations fall into the match category. Some transformations are inherently imperative in style; they tend to require the complex evaluation of data, not simply discovering a text match on an element. For instance, a transformation may require the comparison of vendor prices, and then creating a purchase order based on the selected vendor requires comparative processing of floating decimals.

XML-Based Distributed Computing

e-Business Integration requires a communication channel for delivering information. A common approach with integration servers is to use asynchronous messaging. Some integration architectures couple the use of a JMS message bus with an XML payload.

Application servers, on the hand, typically provide a component model supported by RMI capability. J2EE is an example of the component model that has become a de facto standard for distributed enterprise computing. Many IT organizations have implemented integration projects successfully with CORBA products. Microsoft has touted Distributed COM (DCOM) and MSMQ as mature base technologies for integration, but they work only on the Windows platform.

All these technologies can be leveraged to build the integration transport layer, but there are two primary drawbacks. First, DCOM and CORBA are limited in their capability to seamlessly interoperate across different platforms. Unfortunately, the fact that DCOM works only on Windows limits its use for *enterprise* integration of any kind. (DCOM is available on UNIX, but it has largely been unsuccessful.) CORBA products generally have good coverage of platforms but do not work well with each other. Interoperability with CORBA across enterprises is slow and cumbersome with the use of the Internet Inter-ORB Protocol (IIOP).

IIOP and DCOM carry a second disadvantage. As you've read several times in this book, e-Business Integration involves more than the traditional intra-enterprise EAI. It requires integration beyond the firewalls, and herein lies the problem for both technologies. Firewalls put in place to protect the enterprise from external intrusion do not work well with technologies such as IIOP and DCOM that operate on an open synchronous channel.

What's needed is a distributed Remote Procedure Call (RPC) that is XML-based, platform-independent, and firewall-friendly. That is at the heart of what XML-RPC is all about. Figure 8.6 shows how it is used to integrate between the corporate firewall.

8

LEVERAGING XML
FOR INTEGRATION

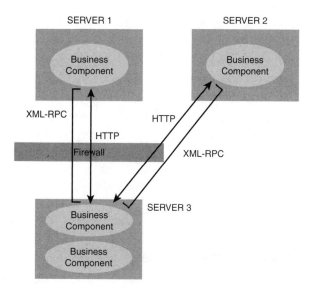

FIGURE 8.6
XML-RPC over Corporate firewall.

You are already familiar with the idea of XML as objects under the DOM model. XML-RPC works well across the firewall because it uses the one protocol that is firewall-friendly—HTTP. In fact, HTTP, as discussed in previous chapters, is still widely used for B2B integration for that very reason. XML-RPC allows a simple HTTP post to be used to deliver a method call to an XML object. It binds together the advantages of XML, RPC, and HTTP to essentially provide a portable, distributed computing mechanism that works well not only within the enterprise, but also beyond.

XML-Based Meta Data

Before I cover how XML is leveraged for meta data, let me first ensure that we're on the same page with regard to our understanding of meta data. Meta data is simply data that describes data: It may describe the ontology, the content, or the structure of the data. Meta data is around us in everyday life. When you search for a book in a library or look in an index at the back of a book, you are using meta data. In the case of integration, meta data provides a description of global enterprise data.

Application integration meta data falls into three categories:

- Application content meta data
- Document/message schema meta data
- Integration rules meta data

Application Content Meta Data

Application content meta data describes the nature of enterprise application data. It varies from application to application. For some applications, it may be little more than the history and version of the data. For other applications, meta data may define the type and intent of each data element. At times, meta data will provide a description of the organization of the data elements or categories in relation to each other. One of the advantages of managing application content meta data in an integration model is that you will develop an ontological model of your enterprise data. In other words, you will understand the type and categorization of data, including where to access this data within the enterprise. This leads to an ability to normalize your integration flows. Sadly, many applications are limited in the provision of meta data.

Document/Message Schema Meta Data

Document/message schema meta data means that XML is used to provide information regarding the structure and organization of application messages externalized for integration. For instance, document schema for a package application like SAP may not be exactly like the IDocs represented internally within the application but rather the externalization of that data as an application message, as shown in Figure 8.7.

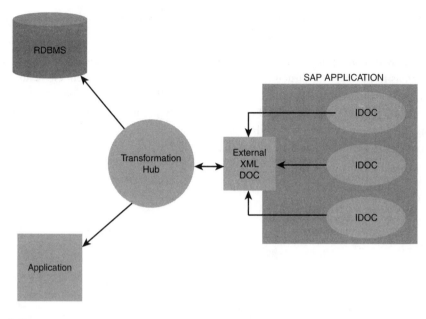

FIGURE 8.7

Example of XML with SAP Application.

The schemas that describe this externalized message are what I refer to as *document schema meta data*. Information regarding the structure and elements of the document is essential to the ability to define the exchange of data.

Integration Rules Meta Data

By integration rules meta data, let me explain that I'm not strictly referring to inference rules. Instead, I use the phrase *integration rules* rather loosely (at least in this particular instance) to describe the data related to mapping, transformation, filtering, and routing the flow of data. Integration rules meta data is the meta data connected with describing the configuration of data flow. It allows you to manage the mappings and configurations by providing information pertaining to the version, dependencies, and historical audits of these integration rules.

XML and Meta Data

How is XML changing and affecting the way meta data is managed? First, applications are beginning to adopt XML not simply as data exchange interfaces but also as a means to describe the application content. The strength of using XML in this manner is obvious. The fact that it is self-describing allows each application to describe its own data in a descriptive language that can be universally parsed and processed. Meta data, after all, is simply data and subject to change as the nature of the application evolves. XML's extensibility permits changes to the meta data to be made easily and without impact.

Second, more and more applications are externalizing data as XML documents. The use of XML Schemas to describe the structure, type, and attributes of the document elements, can provide a level of type safety. Because the DTD is not itself an XML document, it could not be parsed by XML processors and required to be individually processed. With XML Schemas describing the all types of data, the validity of the meta data can be ratified before the actual application document is validated, as shown in Figure 8.8.

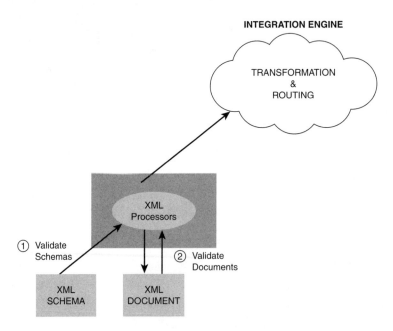

FIGURE 8.8

Validating XML Schema and Document before integrating.

Used in the context of integration, XML Schemas guarantee the integrity of the data flow, beginning with the externalized application document to the mappings between the XML documents. The use of XSLT style sheets extends that kind of validation to the transformation of data as well. The declarative nature of XSLT transformations ensures that as long as the style sheet is validated, the resulting document will essentially be correctly produced. An instruction or imperative style transformation may not result in the correct output because it is not deterministic with regard to the result. In other words, the result is based on *executing defined actions* upon the input as opposed to *declaring* what the output should be through XSLT style sheets.

XML Integration Model

You've discovered how XML can be leveraged to create a new portable model for integration. It does so in the following ways:

- XML documents provide a portable container for application data.
- XML can be used to model relational data as data objects.
- XSLT is a dynamic, declarative transformation engine for transforming XML to any other text-based document.
- XML-RPC offers a distributed computing mechanism for XML objects that works over the Internet and across firewalls.
- XML can be used to capture enterprise application meta data.

When you're discussing XML documents, DOM, XSLT, and XML-RPC, it is valuable to remember that each can be implemented today with available technology. This provides the opportunity to create an XML-centric model for integration, as shown in Figure 8.9.

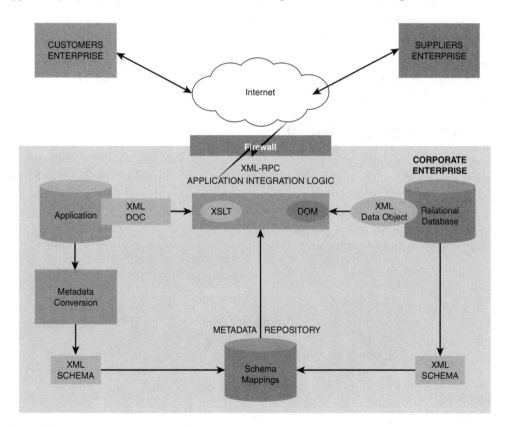

FIGURE 8.9

XML-based Integration Model.

This XML-based integration model is still in its infancy, but it is one that carries great promise for the future. It takes into account the need for inter-enterprise data integration. It supports a portable container for data, dynamic transformations, and a rich meta data model. In coming days, more products will emerge that will do away with proprietary, closed systems in favor of this open integration model.

RosettaNet: An XML-Based Trading Standard

The emphasis for e-Business Integration, especially B2Bi, will evolve from merely the open exchange of XML documents to managed B2B processes. This paves the way for numerous open standards that define a standard for the B2B process in a given domain. For an example, take a brief look at RosettaNet, one of the leading B2B exchange standards today.

Formed in 1998, RosettaNet is an independent consortium with a distinct charter to build a set of B2B interfaces for the information technology and electronics component industry. It spells out the processes necessary for partners in this industry (suppliers, distributors, resellers, manufacturers, and system integrators) to conduct supply chain management. By leveraging XML as a basis for document exchange and defining the processes for B2B interactions, open-standards supply chain management can be realized.

RosettaNet has significant momentum and broad industry support. Among their partners are Cisco, Compaq, Dell, Hewlett-Packard, Intel, Siemens AG, and Sun Microsystems. You can obtain more information about RosettaNet from the Web site at www.rosettanet.org.

The RosettaNet Model

RosettaNet is about defining processes that govern the business transactions between participants in a supply chain. The RosettaNet model for e-Business transactions, illustrated in Figure 8.10, can best be understood as having three primary elements: a Partner Interface Process (PIP), dictionaries, and the RosettaNet Implementation Framework.

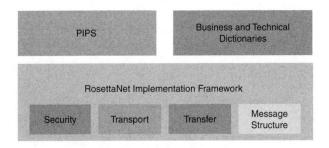

FIGURE 8.10

The RosettaNet model.

RosettaNet PIP

Just in case you're wondering, in this instance, a PIP is not a backup singer for the popular Motown vocalist Gladys Knight. It stands for the Partner Interface Process and is actually the centerpiece of the RosettaNet model. The PIP defines the activities, decisions, and interactions that each e-Business trading participant is responsible for.

As defined by RosettaNet, all PIPs must have a measurable business outcome, must not be proprietary, and must encapsulate a distinct unit of work. For instance, PIP3Ai is a defined specification for the order management process. In particular, this PIP specification outlines in detail the quote and order entry process so that a buyer can request product quotes from a seller. During any part of the process, if a party fails to perform a defined service, the RosettaNet convention renders the business transaction void.

The PIP specification has three primary sections:

- **Business Operational View (BOV)**—Defines in business process terms the business data entities and roles of the participants.
- **Functional Service View (FSV)**—Defines the network component services necessary to execute a PIP. It consists of network component design and network component interactions.
- **Implementation Framework View (IFV)**—Defines the communication protocols and message formats supported by network components.

You can obtain further details about PIPs from the RosettaNet Web site.

Data Dictionaries

Another significant part of the RosettaNet model is the data dictionaries. The RosettaNet data dictionaries define the attributes for PIPs. Two types of dictionaries play a role in defining PIP attributes:

- **Business dictionary**—Defines the business data entities and business properties for a PIP. It is currently in a version 2.0 revision.
- **Technical dictionary**—Defines product categories and properties. Two technical dictionaries are available. The EC Technical Dictionary (ECTD) defines product categories and attributes for the electronic components market. For instance, product definitions for passive devices provide a listing of properties that describe a passive device. The IT Technical Dictionary (ITTD) defines product categories and attributes for IT-related products. The ITTD definitions for IT products are available in various formats, including .xml, .123, and .dtd files. Both the ECTD and ITTD are currently in revision 1.1.

RosettaNet Implementation Framework

The RosettaNet Implementation Framework (RNIF) provides the underlying service protocol for implementing RosettaNet. The defined protocol allows networked applications to participate in RosettaNet and guarantees interoperability between RosettaNet implementations. The most important protocols established by the RNIF include the following:

- **Message structure**—The machine-readable message format for the transmitted RosettaNet message.
- **Transport**—The transmission protocol for how messages will be sent between RosettaNet partners. The defined protocol is HTTP.
- **Transfer**—The way in which the interactions of exchange will take place. It could be transferred directly server-to-server or indirectly via a Web browser interface.
- **Authentication**—The mechanism by which the identities of the sender and receiver of a communication exchange are reliably established. RosettaNet accomplishes this identification by means of SSL V.3 and digital certificates.

RosettaNet will continue to gain momentum with the support of key solution partners such as WebMethods and Extricity, as well as trading partners such as Cisco, HP, Compaq, and Dell. The architects of RosettaNet have correctly focused not simply on business document exchange, but also on creating a framework for business processes to function. With the inclusion of Business Process Integration (BPI) technology applied to this space, an open-standards supply chain will become a reality.

Summary

This chapter looked at the role of XML in e-Business Integration. It introduced the notion of an XML-based integration model founded on five elements:

1. XML as a flexible, extensible container for application data
2. XML as a portable data object model for modeling relational data
3. XSLT as an open transformation language through the use of style sheets
4. XML-RPC as a distributed computing mechanism for the integration transport layer
5. XML as a means for meta data definition through the use of XML extensions such as XML Schemas

The chapter also explored RosettaNet, the leading standard for B2B transactions. The RosettaNet trading standard is fundamentally based on the exchange of XML documents. However, it also highlights the importance of providing more than simply XML documents. The next frontier of B2Bi must address the protocol of trading between the participants, and that's what RosettaNet provides for the Electronic Components and Software trading market. The RosettaNet Partner Interface Process packs define the processes between trading partners.

The next chapter will lead you into a discussion on adapters. e-Business Integration cannot be accomplished without being able to interface with applications, and adapters provide the ability to do so. Although most integration gurus acknowledge the importance of adapters, little has been written to explain what adapters are. Chapter 9, "Using Adapters for Application Data Access," will address this need.

Using Adapters for Application Data Access

"Fools ignore complexity. Pragmatists suffer it....Geniuses remove it."
—*Alan J. Perliss, Epigrams of Programming*

IN THIS CHAPTER

Adapters are about removing complexity. That should be good news because interfacing with applications can be extremely complex. The previous chapters briefly covered the different levels of integration: data, interface, and process. They also explored various technologies such as integration brokers and application servers. However, none of those technologies matter if you cannot get to the data. Integration is predicated on your being able to act on application data, which, in turn, implies the ability to effectively access application data. That's where adapters come in. Adapters, or *connectors* as they are sometimes called, are software components that remove much of the complexity around application access. This chapter will examine the role of adapters in integration, the adapter architecture, and the emergence of a new Java-based specification that promotes uniformity in important aspects of adapter design.

The Role of Adapters in Integration

Like many peripheral technologies that emerge progressively, adapters are not well understood or clearly defined. As far as I know, no one has attempted to provide a definition for an adapter, yet most people who work in the integration arena clearly understand the significance of adapters. Some people have referred to them as *connectors* or even less descriptively as *integration packs*. In part, this lack of definition may be because an adapter seems so straightforward and self-descriptive. At least for the purpose of this book and, in particular, this chapter, here's a concise definition of an adapter:

> A set of software services for connecting and accessing application data. It does so by integrating with the application through the database access, designated APIs or other points of interfaces.

Before continuing, I would like to clarify some terms used in the rest of the chapter. When referring to the application that the adapter will interface with, I will use the term *end application*. If the adapter is writing or updating application data, I may refer to the application as the *target end application* and the adapter as a *target adapter*. The converse is also applied. If the adapter receives or reads application data, I may refer to the application as the *source end application* and the adapter as the *source adapter*. The adapter sits between the end application and the rest of the integration infrastructure, as shown in Figure 9.1. The integration infrastructure may be an integration broker or application server, but the idea is that it represents the rest of the integration architecture where transformations and data routing occur. The data package that the adapter exchanges with the integration infrastructure is referred to as the *transmitted message*. The data package that the adapter exchanges with the end application is known as the *application message*.

Adapters are important to integration for obvious reasons. They provide the necessary capability to exchange data with applications, which is essential in various application integration patterns. Figure 9.2 illustrates adapters used in the *brokering application* pattern covered in

Chapter 3, "e-Business Integration Patterns." In this pattern, the emphasis for adapters is on data access. The adapter runs in process within the application server execution space and allows programmatic access to the application data. Typically, the developer interacts with the application through a Java class acting as a facade for the data. The Java class provides methods to get or set application data elements that the runtime adapter will execute on the application. The brokering components hosted by the application server interact with the end-user applications in a synchronous, request-reply orientation.

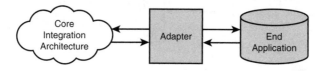

FIGURE 9.1

Adapter mediates between application and integration infrastructure.

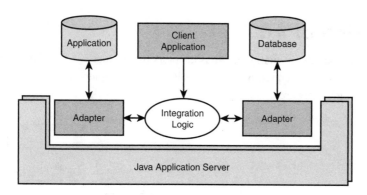

FIGURE 9.2

Brokering application pattern.

An adapter used in conjunction with integration brokers typically functions a little differently. First, it operates as a standalone process that handles application data as messages. Its interaction with the end application is not predicated on synchronous calls from custom code. Instead, as part of an asynchronous event-based system, it receives an application message from a source queue and inserts it into a target queue, as shown in Figure 9.3. In Figure 9.3, also note that it may also conduct specific actions such as applying a filter or translating the data from a transmitted data format to the application-specific format.

One other small difference in both scenarios pertains to the way in which adapters are used. With integration brokers, adapters typically do not need richer semantic control over the data. In other words, adapters used in this fashion require a less extensive set of methods because the interaction is primarily not programmatic. For instance, adapters typically do not need to be functions for deleting data. In most integration broker use cases, data is extracted from and inserted into applications but typically not deleted. However, when they are used with custom-coded components, fine-grained methods for deleting, querying, and browsing data sets are likely to be necessary.

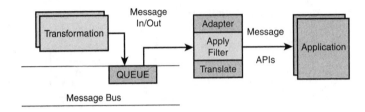

FIGURE 9.3
Adapter working with asynchronous message bus.

Progression of Adapters

As you consider what are normally touted as adapters by product vendors, bear in mind that not all adapters are created equal. As Figure 9.4 illustrates, adapters have progressed from simple APIs to complex software systems.

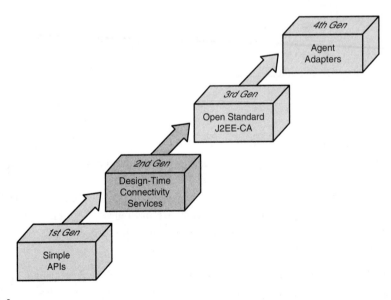

FIGURE 9.4
Progression of adapter technology.

The first generation of adapters emerged out of a need to abstract complex application interfaces from the programmer. From numerous custom-coding engagements to interface with applications and data resources, each vendor began to build proprietary interfaces for common tasks for managing connections, handling errors and transmitting and receiving application messages.

These adapters were simplistic in nature and treated the application or data resource as a black box. They were also largely unsatisfying to the developer using the adapter. Although these adapters provided common APIs for some of the basic functions for application access, they were deficient in a couple of areas.

Examining the insufficiency of these adapters provides insight as to how difficult it is to build adapters that are functionally useful. Much of how each application describes, manages, and externalizes data is proprietary and unique to a given application. Although this first generation of adapters abstracted functions that were commonly used, it didn't really deal with application meta data or identify patterns of usage that enabled a flexible design of adapters.

These limitations led to the emergence of the second generation of adapters, which were more sophisticated. Whereas the first set of adapters were API driven and runtime focused, these newer adapters had a more sophisticated architecture. These adapters were divided into design-time and runtime operations.

The design-time operations allowed for the extraction of the meta data, the mapping of data elements, and were accompanied with tools. Runtime operations provided richer error management and logging facilities as well as connection pooling. In some adapters, transaction handling was also enabled. This use will be described in greater detail in the section on the adapter architecture later in the chapter.

However, even these second-generation adapters had one primary drawback: They were still proprietary in nature and for the most part did not interoperate with other technologies. The adapters from each vendor were somewhat implemented in a proprietary fashion, with no conformity to a common architecture and standard. In fact, the lack of a clear definition led to a blurring of what it means for a vendor to provide adapters. The inability to work with other tools and lack of a common specification limited the use of adapters as an application access technology.

Recent initiatives such as the J2EE Connector Architecture (J2EE-CA) have contributed significantly in defining a third-generation specification. The J2EE-CA promotes a conceptual architecture for a connector. The J2EE connector defines a runtime specification for how adapters will operate with regard to connection management, security, and transaction management. Other aspects of an adapter model are not covered by the specification, but they will be presented later in this chapter. I will also cover J2EE connectors as a specification in greater detail.

Finally, the fourth phase of adapter progression will give rise to agent-adapters that are autonomous and functioning as part of a distributed architecture. It can change the model of integration completely. Agent-adapters extend integration capabilities in node-level processing and direct point-to-point interaction.

Node-Level Processing

With agent-adapters, data processing need not occur simply at a central transformation hub, but at a node level; that is, the adapters function as extreme nodes in the integration infrastructure. Instead of merely interfacing with applications and passing data through, these adapters will be able to process the data. In some situations, this capability may actually be more efficient. For instance, if you want to extract and transform data on employees below the voting age, you can place a filter at the agent-adapter level. This prevents placing data "on the wire" that will just be filtered out at the transformation hub. Rules-based processing applied at the agent-adapter level results in a distributed model of integration that is more efficient and flexible.

Direct Point-to-Point Interaction

Agent-adapters have the facility to conduct point-to-point interactions with each other. Most current adapters do not communicate directly with each other. They transmit data and interact through an intermediary runtime framework provided by a message broker or application server. In most situations, it appears that the central processing hub model will suffice. However, sometimes significant advantages can be gained by agent-adapters being able to directly communicate and invoke each other. To give you an idea of how this may work, consider in Figure 9.5 how a direct point-to-point interaction between two autonomous agent-adapters may be more desirable.

In this example, the agent-adapter for the order management system will send customer order data to the transformation engine in the traditional fashion for processing the order and integrating with the billing system. However, at the same time, that agent-adapter may filter for orders that are greater than $100,000 and generate an invocation of the wireless application protocol (WAP) agent-adapter for wireless notification services. The WAP agent-adapter will trigger a call to the sales agent, indicating that a large order has come in. In this case, simple processing and direct invocation of the agent-adapter result in a more efficient and flexible solution.

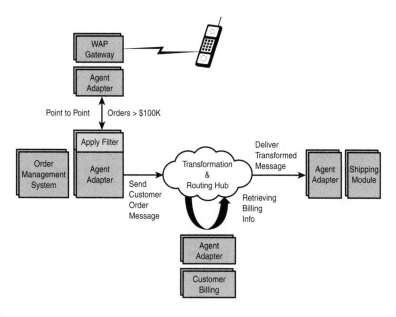

FIGURE 9.5
Agent-adapters in point-to-point interaction.

The Adapter Model

The adapter model, depicted in Figure 9.6, is a conceptual model that identifies the basic components of a fully functional adapter. It defines a boundary between adapter design time and runtime.

Design Time

The adapter design-time components are responsible for defining the application messages that represent the externalized data set. This means being able to access the application and derive application message schemas. Depending on the type of adapter, there may be as many as four design-time components in the adapter model. They are listed below:

- **Configuration tool**—This component is used to enter the physical access parameters for a given data resource. They include the application module instance, session parameters, and login and security profile information.

- **Meta-data extractor**—This component is used to extract application meta data. Meta data is simply information about the application data. The idea behind the meta-data extractor is that you can extract information about data structures or records as defined by the application. For databases, this means being able to retrieve the data dictionaries and schemas. For example, in COBOL applications, it means using what is commonly known as a COBOL copybook utility.

- **Data mapper**—This component is linked closely to the meta-data extractor. After information about the structure of the application data is known, you can then map the application native structures to an externalized message structure that will be the basis for integrating with other applications. Some adapters allow you to define filters and conditional processing rules at this point.

- **Session recorder**—Depending on the technique employed to integrate with the end application, you may require the use of a session recorder. Adapters to some applications actually obtain the data not through a query of meta data and mapping but through simulating a user interaction. This is applied in the User Interface pattern for adapters covered in the section "Adapter Patterns" later in this chapter. This capability is necessary because many mainframe or transactional systems are session driven and the piece of information to be retrieved is several levels down in the user session. To obtain the information, the session recorder records as a user conducts a session of interest and often generates classes that pertain to a particular screen or user session interaction. At runtime, the adapter component executes the generated components, which, in effect, play back and simulate the user session in the same way a user might interact with the application.

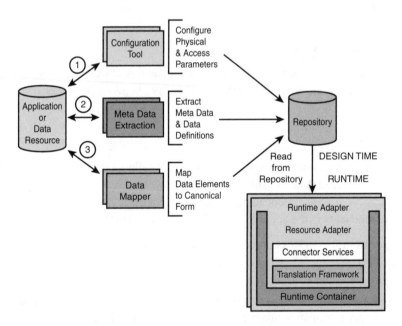

FIGURE 9.6

The adapter model.

Runtime

All user-specified configuration and mapping information at design time is stored in the repository. At runtime, a different set of components takes over, loading the information from the repository at startup. The runtime components are as follows:

- **Connector services**—This component manages connection pooling, security credentials, and transactions. The J2EE-CA proposes an industry specification for connector services that leverages J2EE-based application servers.

- **Resource adapter**—This component contains the code specific to interfacing with the end application. It connects to the application as well as receives, writes, updates, and even deletes application data. For a resource adapter component to accomplish these tasks, it must be able to communicate with applications either through an API or protocol or directly with the database. The SAP resource adapter can interface with SAP through its proprietary interfaces, ALE-IDOC or BAPIs.

- **Translator framework**—Application data is translated between the native data format and the transmitted message format whenever any data is handled between the application and integration infrastructure. Increasingly, this transmitted message format is in XML, although many integration products employ a proprietary message format. A translator framework is required at runtime to perform this translation from application native to transmitted message format and vice versa.

Adapter Patterns

Adapters are as different as the applications they interface with. When you examine adapters, you can see different patterns emerge. Common design patterns are applied in constructing adapters.

Examining these patterns is useful for a couple of reasons. First, you might find that at some point you need to build a custom adapter, and studying adapter design patterns will assist you in that endeavor. Although you can find software vendors building adapters for most of the top applications on the market, there is a "diminishing return" factor in seeking to develop adapters for less-popular applications. This makes it likely that an integration project will necessitate the development of a custom adapter.

Second, understanding adapter patterns can help you understand how adapters work. Even if you purchase off-the-shelf adapters from a vendor, understanding the patterns will assist you in understanding the different approaches that can be applied in constructing an adapter.

9

**USING ADAPTERS
FOR APPLICATION
DATA ACCESS**

The following sections identify six adapter patterns. You can view them as six common design techniques applied in interfacing with applications or data resources. In the following sections, you'll examine these six patterns in greater detail:

- Database Access pattern
- Interface File Exchange pattern
- Remote Method Call pattern
- User Interface (UI) Protocol pattern
- Socket-Queue pattern
- Transactional Proxy pattern

Database Access Pattern

In practice, the Database Access pattern is the most common means of getting to application data. It's ground zero as far as application access is concerned.

In the absence or availability of other techniques, you can generally count on database access as the default means of application access. Although not all applications provide a programmable API, most store data in a relational database. One of the primary reasons for the widespread use of the Database Access pattern is simply the ease of data access through the Structured Query Language (SQL). SQL provides a mechanism for instructions to be structured and issued for data retrieval, updates, and deletes.

The Database Access pattern exists in two forms, differentiated by the manner in which the source adapter receives data from the end application. The first approach uses polling to detect a change in state of data records of interest. A SQL query is issued at regular intervals to determine whether specific data elements that compose an application message have changed. If so, the adapter issues a second SQL query to actually retrieve the application message. Figure 9.7 illustrates an adapter querying to detect a new Customer record added to the database. When one is detected, the adapter issues a second query that pulls together and constructs a Customer_Billing message.

As you might expect, polling is often not a popular choice because it is generally regarded as inefficient. That conclusion may be too sweeping as a generalization. Certain situations are actually conducive to using this technique. If the business scenario does not require low latency but has a high volume of data, using polling may actually be beneficial. In that scenario, a longer polling interval is used, minimizing the likelihood of an *empty poll* (that is, a poll that does not detect a change of state). With some historical analysis, the polling interval can be tuned to ensure that each poll will result in at least n number of new data records fetched. Given the parameters of high latency and high volume, this system can actually be preferable to an event-based system that triggers on each change of state.

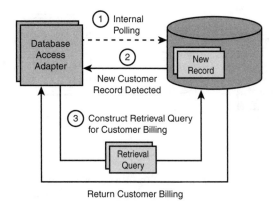

FIGURE 9.7
A database access adapter using polling to receive a message from a source end application.

Having established the legitimacy of the polling technique, it is still likely that most people would prefer an event-based mechanism. Stored procedures are used for this purpose. Stored procedures are executable code that can be triggered when certain events occur within a database. For instance, a stored procedure can be executed to notify the adapter that a new customer has been entered in the database. The adapter then issues the query to retrieve the customer billing message in exactly the same way as it would with the polling technique. The use of stored procedures *triggers* the adapter to issue the query as opposed to having the adapter detect for change.

In general, the Database Access pattern has the advantage of being easy to apply, and as mentioned previously, it is regarded as a default means of access. However, this pattern should come with a warning label. Its disadvantages extend beyond issues of data latency. Because you bypass the application logic and obtain access directly with the database, you run the risk of contaminating the data. Any error will possibly nullify the integrity of the operational database.

Interface File Exchange Pattern

With the Interface File Exchange pattern, the end application provides import/export tables as a means for exchanging data. Like the Database Access approach, this is a commonly applied adapter pattern. Many application vendors frown at the thought of direct access to the database outside the purview of the application code. As an alternative, they make available external tables or files that provide a means for importing and exporting data. Figure 9.8 shows the typical scenario of an adapter utilizing the Interface File Exchange pattern.

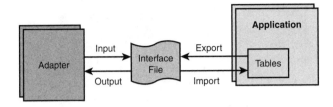

FIGURE 9.8

The Interface File Exchange pattern in action.

An example of an application vendor that employs this approach is Oracle. The Open Interface Table (OIT) provided by the Oracle Applications suite, covered in Chapter 12, "Interfacing with Oracle Applications," is essentially an interface exchange file. The OIT mirrors the data found in the "live" tables.

The benefit of the Interface File Exchange pattern is that it protects the integrity of live data and is generally easy to apply. However, like the Database Access pattern, the fundamental flaw in this approach pertains to the ability to perform low-latency integration where immediacy for data updates is crucial.

Remote Method Call Pattern

The Remote Method Call pattern, which might also be referred to as the Remote API pattern, requires that the application provide a Remote Method Invocation (RMI) type interface for data access. By this, I mean that the adapter utilizing the Remote Method Call pattern may invoke the application's APIs from a separate process and even physically distinct machine. Providing a remote API generally allows for event-based extensions through callbacks. Instead of using polling, a callback method can be invoked for certain changes of state, as illustrated by Figure 9.9.

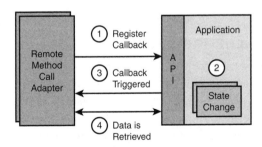

FIGURE 9.9

The Remote Method Call pattern with callbacks.

The support for an API varies from application to application. Some applications such as SAP provide significant support for programmable interfaces through their Remote Function Call (RFC) or Business API (BAPI) interfaces. Others such as Oracle tend to provide little support for RPC-based integration APIs.

User Interface Protocol Pattern

Adapters utilizing the User Interface (UI) Protocol pattern obtain access to the application data through the user interface. In other words, the adapter interacts with the end application through the same mechanism as a user would. This pattern is commonly applied for access to legacy applications. All mainframe user sessions are driven through this protocol. As an example, a TN3270 protocol adapter would, in essence, emulate the user interaction required to retrieve and input application data. An example is shown in Figure 9.10. The adapter would generate components that emulated the specific user interactions through techniques that are generically known as *screen scraping* or *screen stuffing*.

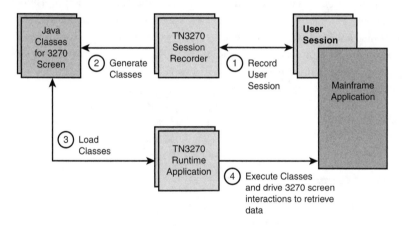

FIGURE 9.10

The User Interface Protocol pattern.

The TN5250 protocol for the AS/400 is another example of applicability for this pattern. Although it may seem primitive for the B2B arena, HTML scrapping and stuffing are still widely used as a means of data exchange. The HTML adapter interacts with application data through a thin client-to-server interface.

One of the primary benefits of the UI Protocol pattern is that data is accessed in a relatively safe manner. Unlike database access adapters, the adapter that is designed in the UI Protocol pattern interacts with the application data without bypassing the application logic. In a sense, it operates within the "sandbox" of what is permissible through the user session. In other words, the adapter can do only what is permissible for the user to do through the user interface. An example of the application logic that governs this sandbox is the error management and validations that are part of the user session. The UI protocol adapter application messages that are entered as part of the adapter-simulated session are validated by the same code as well.

Socket-Queue Pattern

Some applications provide a socket or message queue as a point of asynchronous interface with external systems. The Socket-Queue pattern takes advantage of this interface point by placing target application messages into the socket/queue and receiving source application messages on the socket/queue. As with the other patterns, receiving source application messages proves to be the more interesting challenge. In this pattern, the adapter essentially provides a listener component. The listener component may poll the socket/queue, but often a more compelling approach is to use a callback facility within a queuing system. This can be accomplished by subscribing through a publish-subscribe system, as shown in Figure 9.11. With a publish-subscribe system, the adapter, acting as a messaging client registers for a topic (in Java Messaging Service vernacular, this is called a *topic* rather than a *queue* so I'll use that term here). Topics are message typed—that is, there is one topic for a given type of message. When the messaging system receives a message of a given type, it automatically delivers that message to all adapters that are registered for that topic.

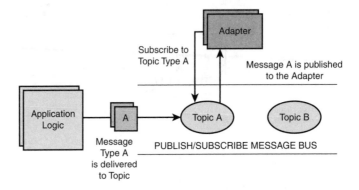

FIGURE 9.11

The Socket-Queue pattern at work.

Package applications generally do not provide a socket or message queue interface, but often this can be helpful in accessing custom applications that use asynchronous messaging. This is particularly true of applications that use MQ Series as a messaging backbone.

Transactional Proxy Pattern

Just as messaging-based applications are best accessed through the Socket-Queue pattern, some applications hosted in a transaction processing monitor (TPM) are best accessed through a transactional pattern adapter. TPMs are the forerunner to the Java-based application servers of today. A TPM such as CICS on the mainframe or Tuxedo on UNIX provides an execution environment for application code. This means that memory management, error handling, security, and transactions are handled by the TPM runtime.

The transactional proxy adapter actually interacts with the application through a TPM proxy. For distributed TPMs like Tuxedo, the proxy is actually a Tuxedo client that interfaces with the TPM server through a defined set of interfaces known as the Application Transaction Monitor Interface (ATMI). Through ATMI, the adapter can open or close application resources, manage transaction boundaries, and allocate or free buffers. For host-centric TPMs like CICS, a gateway service acts as the proxy to the TPM. For instance, CICS provides a Java Transaction Server gateway for external Java applications to access CICS data. However, in the event that the adapter is not written in Java (either by choice or necessity), a proxy that interfaces through the standard External Call Interface (EXCI) is required. The architecture of the transactional proxy pattern applied for CICS is shown in Figure 9.12.

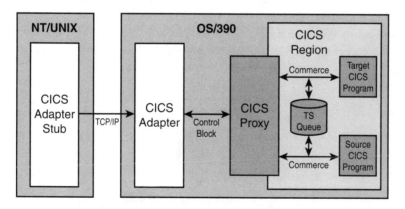

FIGURE 9.12
Transactional Proxy pattern for CICS.

The J2EE Connector Architecture

It is worthwhile to take a little detour to discuss the recent introduction of the J2EE Connector Architecture. The J2EE Connector Architecture (J2EE-CA) specification may be one of the least-known elements of the J2EE platform, but it is important nonetheless. J2EE-CA proposes a common mechanism for J2EE application servers to manage application connectivity in a consistent, scalable, and secure fashion. In practice, this equates to the following benefits:

- Application developers have a common way of accessing various enterprise applications.
- Application servers supply rich services to support enterprise application connectivity.
- Instead of the proprietary application adapters that proliferate today, the J2EE-CA provides a basis for interoperable connectors running within a J2EE platform.

In short, J2EE-CA makes it easier to provide connectors by providing system-level interoperability between the J2EE application server and Enterprise Information System (EIS). EIS is simply a J2EE moniker for enterprise resources such as applications, databases, or even transaction monitors. Without J2EE-CA today, connectors are developed to link a specific application server to a specific EIS. On the other hand, with J2EE-CA, connectors for a given EIS work with any number of J2EE-compliant application servers.

How Do J2EE Connectors Work?

To understand how J2EE connectors work, you need to understand the different elements in the J2EE-CA model depicted in Figure 9.13. The resource adapter is the component that has EIS-specific interface code. For example, the SAP resource adapter contains code that accesses the SAP through its proprietary BAPI interface. The J2EE-CA also establishes a number of system-level contracts between the application server and resource adapter. These contracts define interoperability between the application server and application resource adapter.

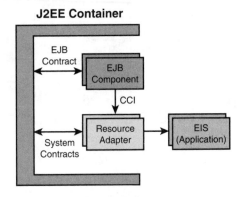

FIGURE 9.13

Simplified View of J2EE Connector Architecture.

The Common Client Interface (CCI) provides an RPC-enabled client-side API for accessing the enterprise systems. In other words, if you write business logic components that require application access, you use CCI to interact with the EIS. In fact, the CCI provides APIs to do the following:

- Manage the EIS connectivity (for example, the `getConnection` method)
- Conduct interactions with EIS
- Manage EIS meta data

I won't go into the details of the CCI in this chapter, but if you're intrigued to learn more, refer to Chapter 9 of the Java Connector Architecture specification document.

Application Server Managing the Resource Adapter

The J2EE-CA model defines standard operating mechanisms between the application server and J2EE connector's resource adapter. Each mechanism is predicated on tight system-level interactions between the application server and resource adapter. As an example, look at how interactions between the application server and resource adapter function when a connection request is made.

When a connection is requested by the client application through the CCI, the resource adapter passes the request to the application server. The application server services the request through its connection manager. The connection manager first references the connection pool. If a connection is available for use, the connection manager returns a handle to the adapter. If no connection is available, the connection manager invokes the managed connection factory in the resource adapter to create a new physical connection. Figure 9.14 shows an example of J2EE connectors at work.

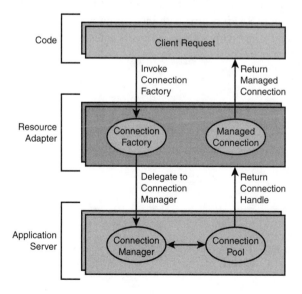

FIGURE 9.14

J2EE Connectors at Work with J2EE Application Server.

9

USING ADAPTERS
FOR APPLICATION
DATA ACCESS

The J2EE-CA model also defines other standard mechanisms to manage transactions, security certificates, and deployment packages. It also ensures facilities for error management and logging, which is an often-overlooked but critical element of enterprise integration infrastructure.

Summary

In this chapter, you learned about the important role adapters play in integration. This chapter covered a lot of ground, including discussions of the progression of adapters and adapter architecture. In exploring the adapter architecture, you discovered the basic functional components of the adapter architecture. Later in the chapter, you also learned about the six primary adapter patterns:

- Database Access
- Interface File Exchange
- Remote Method Call
- UI Protocol
- Socket-Queue
- Transactional Proxy

The advantages and disadvantages of each were also discussed. Finally, you were introduced to the emerging J2EE Connector Architecture standard.

The next chapter begins a series of five chapters on integrating with specific applications. Chapter 10, "Interfacing with SAP," begins with interfacing with SAP. It will provide you with a keen sense for how to integrate with SAP, should your integration project warrant it.

Adapting to Applications

IN THIS PART

Interfacing with SAP

"If I had my life to live over again, I'd be a plumber."
—Albert Einstein (1879-1955)

IN THIS CHAPTER

SAP has distinguished itself as the leading provider of enterprise resource planning (ERP) systems for Global 2000 companies. Although known for ERP systems, SAP has application modules for other critical business functions spanning from accounting to sales automation. It also addresses numerous vertical industries, including manufacturing, banking, utilities, and education. In many ways, SAP represents the 800-pound gorilla of the package applications space. Therefore, a discussion of application integration wouldn't be complete without covering SAP R/3 integration. This chapter discusses the SAP application suite in broad strokes. It also examines the technology interfaces and addresses basic approaches to integrating with SAP.

Overview of SAP R/3 Application Suite

SAP R/3 is the most current SAP application suite deployed today. It runs on many platforms, is highly customizable, and provides enterprise scalability.

In the ERP space, SAP has always been the leader in providing APIs and tools to enable integration of their systems and modules to other legacy systems. The most recent release of SAP R/3, Release 4.6C, adds to the list of available interface mechanisms. The most widely known interface mechanisms in SAP R/3 are the ALE/IDocs. Believe it or not, this is one of the simplest forms of data (document) exchange in SAP. The later versions of SAP (release 4.0 and higher) have a newer, more technologically advanced interface mechanism known as the Business Application Programming Interface, or BAPI. This chapter discusses both of these interface mechanisms in some detail. It also briefly discusses other points of integration available within SAP R/3.

Recently, SAP released its e-Business extension of the R/3 application suite under the mySAP.com banner. mySAP was conceived with the intention of capturing and defining the Internet business environment. However, since its release in May 2000, it has yet to realize the vision of the SAP e-Business network of collaborative services. Nonetheless, it represents the future of SAP's vision and warrants a brief discussion. The major components of the e-Business application suite include the following:

mySAP Workplace—Provides a customized portal for users (employees) of an organization

mySAP Marketplace—Enables development of open or closed marketplaces with buying and selling capabilities, including B2B procurement, RFP/RFQ, and so on

mySAP CRM—Provides Internet-enabled customer relationship management (CRM) capable of generating sales leads, support for customer service centers, and so on

mySAP Supply Chain Management—Provides collaboration with partners and management of back office operations

The SAP e-Business Suite is differentiated by its applications' readiness to be managed by an external hosting or application service provider (ASP) environment. SAP has recognized the emergence of the ASP as a delivery mechanism for business systems to smaller and mid-sized organizations.

SAP R/3 Integration

My coauthor and I recently solicited comments from a group of knowledgeable developers on the challenge of integrating with SAP. The results might surprise you. We got responses ranging from "relatively straightforward" to "excruciating." If you assume that most of the developers were somewhat equally competent, the reason for these responses may be due to the dichotomy faced in attempting to integrate with a SAP system. On one hand, integrating with SAP is relatively straightforward because SAP supplies a more robust set of integration APIs and protocols compared to the other major application vendors. There are also numerous training courses and materials on SAP to help facilitate the learning process. On the other hand, SAP is, in general, more difficult to install and run. It's not to be undertaken without an experienced consultant by your side. Add to this the complexity of understanding the SAP architecture and its perceived convoluted meta data, and it comes as no surprise that many consider SAP systems difficult to integrate with. This chapter provides a broad overview of the interface mechanisms available within SAP R/3 to integrate with external third-party applications. The chapter does not discuss the intricacies of installing or operating SAP because that topic is worthy of a separate book and is addressed by many excellent publications.

ALE Overview

The ALE/IDoc interfaces provide a reliable and secure communication mechanism for distributed data exchange. ALE, which is an acronym for Application Link and Enabling, is deemed the preferred way for SAP application modules to exchange data. ALE has been available as part of the SAP application infrastructure since version 3.0. It is actually a messaging infrastructure provided by SAP R/3; it allows for the exchange of business data between two SAP processes. The original idea behind ALE is to enable effective peer-to-peer exchange of SAP application information. Through the use of ALE, physically distinct SAP systems can exchange business data seamlessly as part of a logical business process. However, its use has extended beyond simply transmission of information between SAP systems. Just as often, the ALE/IDoc interface is also used as a standard communication channel for SAP systems to link with other third-party applications.

The primary objective of ALE is to guarantee a distributed yet fully integrated R/3 installation. The ALE architecture can be segmented into three layers, as shown in Figure 10.1.

The communication layer establishes the communication channel for data delivery. It allows the user to set appropriate communication parameters, depending on the system that it is communicating with. This layer is the foundation of SAP R/3 integration mechanisms. One of the basic components of this layer is the Remote Function Call (RFC), which enables remote calls (access) to SAP functions from other systems. RFC is a proprietary infrastructure originally designed by SAP to enable communications between more than one instance of SAP systems.

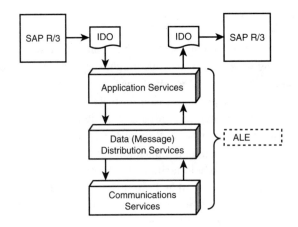

FIGURE 10.1

ALE architecture.

The data distribution layer enables the coupling of distributed business applications. It does so by providing three essential services:

- Determining recipients of data based on a data distribution model
- Filtering and conversion of messages
- Data/message compression for increased performance

The application layer provides an interface to the R/3 system to generate and receive messages containing data to or from other R/3 or external systems. Messages contain routing information such as the name of the recipient, the type of transmission to use, and the rules to apply for processing IDocs.

If you're used to managing distributed infrastructures, you can relate to the difficulties of modeling the distributed components of a large system. SAP is no exception. Planning the distributed environment is an important step in the implementation process. The ALE architecture enables system architects and analysts to represent the entire SAP system needs in a logical model. This logical model specifies the topology or, in simpler terms, defines which application should run on which physical systems and how the systems should exchange data. SAP comes with a reference model for distributing applications in various feasible scenarios. These scenarios can be customized to suit specific implementation requirements.

ALE architecture replaced its predecessor, the Batch Data Communication (BDC). The BDC, as the name indicates, was not a middleware technology but rather a batch processing protocol for data exchange. As with most batch protocols, limitations with error handling, systems management, and security became a problem. ALE now replaces BDC and provides the robust middleware architecture that is necessary for SAP to non-SAP communication.

Why use ALE/IDoc? This established protocol has four primary benefits. First, the ALE layer acts as an abstraction from the SAP application layer. This means that SAP ensures that the ALE technology will resolve any issues resulting from a version upgrade and maintain backward compatibility. It is also the reason why even though ALE was originally developed for SAP-to-SAP communication, it functions identically for SAP to non-SAP communication. The ALE middleware is unaware of either the sender or receiver systems.

The second benefit of ALE is that the ALE messaging infrastructure ensures "once and only once" guaranteed delivery of messages. This means that ALE ensures that once the sender transmits the IDoc, the receiver is guaranteed to receive it. ALE implements a loose "store and forward" facility to ensure that messages always reach their destination even in situations in which the receiver may not be ready to accept the message or the physical connection is disrupted because of network failure. In those situations, ALE buffers the transmitted message and retries until the message is delivered. The "once and only once" tag means that the receiver is guaranteed not to receive multiple copies of the same message.

An additional benefit provided by the ALE technology includes IDoc data management facilities. These facilities allow for the streamlined distribution of IDoc data by providing features such as IDoc Reduction, IDoc Version Management, and IDoc Data Filtering. IDoc Reduction means that the SAP user/developer may choose to customize the IDoc type by eliminating segments of the IDoc that are not used in a given deployment. This is known as "reducing an IDoc" and ensures that the IDoc will contain only the relevant data subset. IDoc Version Management simply means that the IDocs and individual message segments are version-controlled for distribution or processing. IDoc Filtering allows for the dynamic reduction of an IDoc instance. At runtime, either complete IDocs or certain message segments within an IDoc can be removed before delivery of the IDoc.

Finally, ALE provides systems management capabilities that allow for start/restart/recovery of the ALE system. It also enhances the management of the integration solution by providing error handling built into the ALE layer. This is important because the ability for an integration interface to reliably analyze the transmission of information and provide exception handling is critically important. ALE provides the kind of management capability that is necessary for integrating SAP with other third-party systems.

IDoc Overview

As for the other half of the ALE/IDoc protocol, IDoc stands for Intermediate DOCument. IDoc is a proprietary data package or container defined by SAP for data exchange. It can contain any desired R/3 application data. It is an "externalized" data format in the sense that it doesn't reflect the database structures within SAP at all. IDocs have been broadly used as part of the SAP-EDI data exchanges. Despite the popularity of B2B and XML, the reality is that EDI has been used for decades as a means of transacting business between corporations. Typically, when SAP systems have interfaced with EDI subsystems, it has been via the IDoc data

10

exchange format. Hence, it probably comes as no surprise to discover that IDoc is loosely based on EDI standards, in particular the EDIFACT standard.

IDocs are character based and are human readable. The term *human readable* is really loose because unless you are extremely familiar with a given IDoc type, the fact that you can read the IDoc in no way implies that you can understand its structure. The contents generally don't make sense due to the complexity, convoluted names, and sheer volume of data fields.

Generally, the structure of R/3 tables used for the physical storage of IDoc is referred to as the *external structure*, and the description of the structure of the application data contained in the tables is referred to as the *internal structure* of the IDoc. I will discuss both the external structure as well as the internal structures of the IDoc before getting into the details of how to use ALE/IDoc mechanism for integrating your legacy systems with SAP R/3.

The external IDoc structure has three record types:

Control record—The control record acts as a fixed header record defined by SAP. It contains information about the IDoc, such as the IDoc type, sender/receiver information, as well as a unique identifier for that IDoc instance. The structure of the control record is identical for all IDocs.

Data record—The data record contains two components or segments: the administrative component and data component. The administrative component uniquely identifies a segment such as segment name, segment number, hierarchy level, and so on. The data component is simply a byte stream capable of holding any segment structure.

Status record—An IDoc can also contain one or more status records. Status records track the progress of the IDoc as it is processed at different points within the data flow. At each key point within the process flow, a status record is registered within the IDoc containing the status code and a date-time stamp. This means that as the IDoc moves through the various systems, the time, status, and error/warning condition at each point can be monitored.

Each IDoc is organized and identified internally by a sequence of certain segments or segment groups, with each segment containing a number of data records.

Usually, a segment group consists of a header segment (for example, general vendor data) followed by detail segments (for example, bank details of the vendor) at the next hierarchy level. Every IDoc conforms to a predefined internal structure that is shown in Figure 10.2.

Although this chapter discusses IDoc in conjunction with ALE, it is simply a data container and can be used in various other situations. As you learned earlier, IDocs were originally used for EDI in SAP systems. When the application messages are packaged within an IDoc, information is transmitted between the SAP module and the EDI system. Furthermore, translators are provided to map legacy mainframe data to IDoc formats.

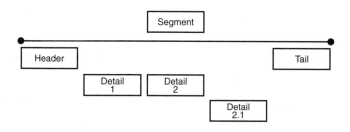

FIGURE 10.2
IDoc structure.

Messages are discrete business events or records transmitted and exchanged between two applications. Examples of application messages include Invoice, Customer, or Sales_Order. Like other applications, SAP modules externally represent critical business data as application messages contained within an IDoc for transmission. A single IDoc contains multiple related messages that share common information. For that reason, an IDoc is not considered to be a message but rather a container or package for multiple messages. For instance, the Customer IDoc type may contain several related messages such as Customer_Billing_Info and Customer_Shipping_Info. Both messages share certain common data elements as part of the Customer IDoc type. Figure 10.3 shows the structure of an IDoc containing multiple message types.

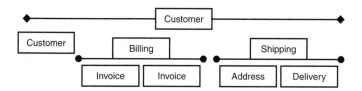

FIGURE 10.3
Multiple messages derived from the IDoc type.

Of course, when communicating between SAP systems as part of a workflow, IDocs can be described as workflow business objects. These objects are stored and managed in the Business Object Repository (BOR). You'll learn more about the BOR when BAPI interfaces are discussed later in this chapter.

Working with ALE/IDoc

Now equipped with an understanding of ALE and IDoc, you are ready to look at how they work together to transmit and receive information to and from SAP. The best way to understand how ALE/IDoc works is to examine it in terms of an outbound ALE process and inbound ALE process.

Outbound ALE Process

An outbound ALE process involves delivering data from a SAP system to other systems. Figure 10.4 shows how the outbound ALE process works. This process is actually fairly simple and can be described in four basic steps:

1. **An application trigger event occurs**—This initial step occurs when some event is triggered within SAP to necessitate the transmission of data. This event may be a change of state of a business object, a user-initiated activity, or an occurrence to the database. Any of these activities causes the outbound data process to begin, which essentially means that the data to be delivered is prepared.

2. **A master IDoc is generated**—The master IDoc is the document containing the data to be sent. The data is formatted into the IDoc format as part of the preparation for data delivery. This master IDoc is essentially a master template of all the data that can be sent.

3. **A communication IDoc is generated**—In this step, individual IDocs, known as *communication IDocs*, are generated for each recipient from the master IDoc. Each recipient receives an IDoc with relevant data that may be a subset of the master IDoc. Unlike the master IDoc, each communication IDoc is persisted to a database.

4. **The IDoc is transmitted**—The appropriate IDoc version is delivered to each recipient using an asynchronous communication mode.

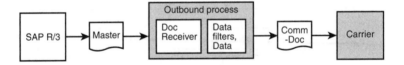

FIGURE 10.4
Outbound data process.

The preceding four steps capture the simplicity of the invocation, generation, packaging, and delivery of IDoc data to the destination systems. This process is elegantly simple and consistently reliable.

Inbound ALE Process

The inbound ALE process occurs when the SAP system receives an IDoc from an external source. The inbound ALE process is remarkably simple as shown in Figure 10.5. The steps revolve around the storage of the incoming IDoc, the invocation of the posting program, and the creation of the application system document.

The beauty of the inbound ALE process is that it is consistent irrespective of the recipient (target) system being another instance of SAP R/3 or an external system.

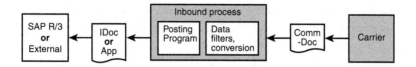

FIGURE 10.5

Inbound ALE process.

The three fundamental steps of an inbound ALE process resulting in the creation of a document in the SAP application are as follows:

1. **The IDoc is stored**—When an IDoc is received from another program, the IDoc is first persisted to a database, and then the syntax and validity of the IDoc are verified.

2. **The posting program reads the IDoc**—A posting program reads the data from the IDoc and creates a SAP system message from that information. There may be a posting program for each message type in an IDoc.

3. **A system document is created**—The posting program creates a system document based on the information in the IDoc. The resulting information is placed in the IDoc.

Understanding BAPI

Object-oriented technology was introduced to SAP R/3 users in Release 3.0 in the form of defined business objects. Access to these business objects in the BOR is possible through the Business Application Programming Interface, also known simply as BAPI. Together, the SAP business object types and their BAPIs provide an object-oriented view of the SAP R/3 business functionality. These business objects and the BAPIs are stored in the BOR.

Learning and understanding SAP business objects are prerequisites to any discussion of BAPI. SAP business objects encapsulate real-world data and processes. For example, an employee or a sales order would be represented as a business object and stored in the BOR. A fundamental part of the object-oriented technology is the concept of a *class*. In the SAP R/3 world, a class is known as an *object type*. Each individual business object belongs to a specific object type. The structure of an object type is composed of the following components:

- **Basic data**—These are common properties of all object types such as the unique identifier for the object and default methods.

- **Interfaces**—These are essentially methods, events and attributes of an SAP Business Object.

- **Key fields**—The key fields in SAP function in the same way key fields work in relational databases. They represent fields that uniquely identify an instance of an instance of an object. This allows you to reference and retrieve the object instance.

- **Methods**—A method is an interface for an SAP Business Object that allows to programmer to perform operations on the object. Such operations may include setting attribute values or accessing a data element.
- **Attributes**—An attribute is a data element that describes the object characteristics.
- **Events**—An event is a notification mechanism. It is triggered to notify of a change of status in an SAP Business Object.

Using the SAP-DCOM Interface

SAP first introduced the SAP-DCOM interface in August 1998. Desktop integration is part of most ERP implementations. Integrating data from processes hosted on servers with desktop applications has been a challenge since database servers and client server computing became mainstream architectures.

The DCOM connector unites the SAP business framework with the Windows platform by enabling access to R/3 data as DCOM objects. With the DCOM connector, desktop users can access R/3 data through various mechanisms, including the following:

Programming languages such as Visual Basic and C++ without requiring runtime access to the BOR

DHTML using VBScript or JavaScript

Active Server Pages (ASPs) using VBScript or JavaScript

Encapsulating R/3 data as DCOM objects also enables easy integration with other desktop applications such as Microsoft Office. In the preceding section, you learned how BAPI provides access to SAP business objects stored in the BOR. The DCOM connector is another mechanism to access to the same SAP business objects. Because DCOM is a widely accepted standard compared to BAPI, which is a proprietary technology, the DCOM connector opens up several possible integration scenarios to SAP business objects.

The DCOM connector technology has two basic modules. One module is for administration of the DCOM connector. The other module is for generating DCOM proxy components for SAP business objects. The generated proxy DCOM component is in C++. Regardless of the particular business object it represents, each generated component has the following properties, which it inherits from a super class:

Client—The R/3 client system to be accessed

UserID—The R/3 user account

Password—The password for the user account

Language—The language the R/3 system uses

Destination—The name of a preconfigured destination with associated values that can be selectively overridden by the preceding four properties

Each generated component also features the following methods (the first three of which are inherited from super classes):

PutSessionInfo()—Sets all four destination parameters in a single call.

AdviceRfcGuiSink()—Used if the underlying R/3 function module requires a SAPGUI or used for debugging function modules.

CommitWork()—Used for BAPIs doing database updates without implicit commit.

InitKeys()—Initializes an instance of the DCOM object with particular values for key fields. (No check is performed to see whether an object with those values actually exists in the R/3 database.)

DimAs()—Returns a Microsoft advanced data object(ADO) recordset. These Fields can be accessed with the same names used to access the equivalent ABAP table or structure. This is used to populate data structures that require values before being passed to a BAPI.

Additional generated component methods are derived from the definition of the R/3 business object. Business object methods are duplicated in the generated component. The method's original name is preceded by Bapi; for instance, the ExistenceCheck() method of the Employee object becomes BapiExistenceCheck(). Key fields of the business object become retrievable properties of the generated component with their names preceded by Key; for example, Number becomes KeyNumber.

The components the DCOM connector generates are *dual-interface*, which means you can use them directly from scripting languages such as Visual Basic and access them remotely from a client without the need for any marshalling DLLs.

Proxy components for BAPIs return tables as ADO recordsets, which support client-side cursors for stepping through the table a row at a time, skipping to a particular row, and even filtering out rows based on field values.

Using DCOM Components on Microsoft Transaction Server (MTS)

The components created by the DCOM connector can be run in the context of MTS. Some of the MTS services not found in the conventional DCOM components include connection pooling, security, and two-phase commit.

Connection Pooling

MTS allows components to share and reuse resources, such as database connections, thus avoiding the overhead associated with creating and destroying these resources. For DCOM connector, SAP has written an MTS resource dispenser that pools the RFC connections to the R/3 system. When a proxy component is created, the component is given the use of a connection from the pool. When the object is destroyed, the RFC context for the connection is wiped clean and returned to the pool. RFC connections don't have to be repeatedly created and destroyed. You can increase application efficiency even more by always making sure that you release proxy component objects as soon as possible (returning their connection resource to the pool).

Security

The MTS management console allows you to define roles, which are sets of users, and groups that are granted access to all components in the package for which that role is defined. This capability gives you additional options for the application security design. For instance, you could configure your DCOM connector component to use a hard-wired destination with a given R/3 user ID and password and then control access to that component with MTS roles.

Two-Phase Commit

New functionality in Microsoft's COM+ will enable future versions of the DCOM connector to support a two-phase commit, allowing more efficient pooling of RFC connections. With a two-phase commit, connections can be allocated just for the duration of a remote method call rather than for the entire lifetime of a component.

You might be wondering about the transaction functionality provided by MTS. Well, strangely enough, the DCOM connector doesn't use any MTS transaction features yet. Before making use of the transaction features, SAP will have to establish a consistent object model between the R/3 and MTS. Until then, the DCOM connector proxy objects will have the transaction feature turned off.

However, even without the full support of MTS features, the DCOM connector plays an important role in opening up SAP business objects to desktop applications. It remains to be seen how this integration mechanism will be used in the real world. Initially, it appears that many IT organizations are still unwilling to use this connector, primarily due to concerns about MTS scalability.

Summary

As is apparent from the discussion so far, there are several methods of exchanging data between SAP systems and between SAP and external systems. SAP has been known to be a very flexible system, capable of being customized to suit some of the most demanding implementations. However, heavy customization results in difficulties during data exchanges. The primary reason for more than one method of integration within SAP is the fact that as SAP functionality increased over the years, so did the requirement for integration. Don't expect to see a drastic change in this situation. Already with the release of mySAP.com, you will see more types of integration mechanisms based on Internet standards. Picking the right mechanism for integrating your applications and business process is the challenge some integration product vendors have solved.

Interfacing with PeopleSoft 8

CHAPTER

11

IN THIS CHAPTER

Just as the name SAP for many years was synonymous with enterprise resource planning (ERP), PeopleSoft is best known as the *de facto* corporate Human Resource Management System (HRMS). In recent years, PeopleSoft has extended its reach as a supplier of enterprise application suites covering HRMS, ERP, and customer relationship management (CRM). With PeopleSoft Version 8.0, it has an opportunity to project a new image and be known for far more than HRMS. According to PeopleSoft, this latest release represents an investment of more than $500 million, development of 60 new applications, and the reconstruction of 108 core products. As with all ambitious initiatives, only time will tell if PeopleSoft has succeeded in establishing a new identity. This chapter discusses the advancements in the product offerings from an integration perspective. At the core of the PeopleSoft integration focus is the Open Integration Framework (OIF) technology.

Like many of the other leading application vendors, PeopleSoft has tried to craft its OIF integration architecture based on the Internet and the need to make e-Business deployments easy. To that effect, each PeopleSoft 8 application is delivered completely in HTML, with no code on the client. However, all the new features and functions haven't eliminated the need for integration between PeopleSoft and other packaged or legacy applications. PeopleSoft customers may well decide to deploy PeopleSoft as their strategic system, but rarely has any organization been able to completely replace old systems with new. Many of those efforts are a study in careful technology evolution. Furthermore, those that have succeeded over a period of time in replacing legacy applications are often awakened to the realization that the rate of technology innovation has rendered their new strategic systems as legacy.

Over the years, architectures have tended to swing between distributed and centralized software paradigms. Although the Internet enables free flow of information and the promotion of open systems, it leans toward server-side architectures. The server-based PeopleSoft Internet architecture leverages ubiquitous, accessible Internet technologies such as XML and HTTP. The primary objective of the PeopleSoft 8.0 reconstruction was to streamline integration among PeopleSoft application modules, legacy systems, B2B trading systems, and other emerging e-Business applications. The three primary components of this architecture are as follows:

- Application messaging
- Component interfaces
- Business interlinks

In the following sections of this chapter, I will discuss in detail all these components and the framework that holds them together. I will begin with an overview of the Internet architecture, which will set the stage for a closer look at the Open Integration Framework. My intention in providing this overview is to give you the necessary information to understand and pick the correct points of integration and apply the appropriate technology for integrating PeopleSoft version 8 with other systems.

Overview of PeopleSoft Internet Architecture

Understanding the Internet architecture requires basic knowledge of some of the principles of Internet and especially Web technology. One unique aspect of Web applications is the nonexistence of application code on client machines. These clients are sometimes known as *zero footprint clients*. This paradigm is achieved by hosting all user interfaces on a server (Web server) and has been extended to the wireless world by the Wireless Application Protocol (WAP) and Wireless Markup Language (WML) technologies. In the Internet-based, B2B world, client access is achieved by exchanging XML documents. The common thread in all three cases is the existence of a server that hosts all client interfaces.

Regardless of the type of client and access mechanism used, each client accesses a set of PeopleSoft application services hosted on a Tuxedo server. Tuxedo is the leading transaction monitor capable of managing transaction states. The PeopleSoft Tuxedo-enabled application services interface with the LDAP server to access security services and a database server to access RDBMS databases. One difference in PeopleSoft's use of RDBMS technology is the storage of PeopleSoft meta data along with the operational data.

The PeopleSoft application server depicted in Figure 11.1 can be one homogenous server, such as BEA WebLogic, or it can be two separate servers (a Web server and Tuxedo server). In either case, the Jolt interface from BEA is required to integrate the different servlets with the application services. A *servlet* is a Java program hosted and launched by a Java-enabled Web server. Three servlets are provided as part of the architecture: Presentation Relay, Portal, and Integration Relay. The Presentation Relay servlet is aimed at creating outbound HTML pages and parsing inbound HTML pages before generating messages to trigger the appropriate application services. The Portal servlet handles personalization of HTML and WML interfaces, content management, and search engine capabilities. However, of the three servlets, the Integration Relay servlet is of special interest for the purposes of this discussion because it enables integration with external systems.

The Integration Relay servlet handles inbound and outbound HTML/XML requests. It is a very thin layer between the external systems and back-end integration services hosted on the Tuxedo server. It receives and serves XML requests over HTTP and maps the data in these requests to the integration services.

The use of servlets keeps the architecture thin and simple. Over the long run, simple architectures are easier to maintain. It is obvious from Figure 11.1 that there are many components in the PeopleSoft application server. The OIF focuses on a subset of these components relevant to application integration.

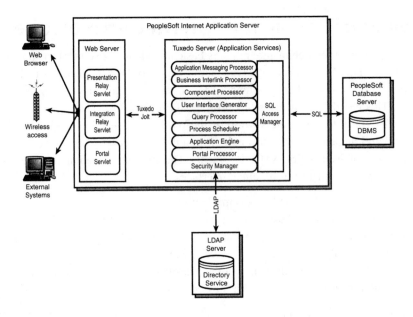

FIGURE 11.1
PeopleSoft application architecture.

Understanding Open Integration Framework (OIF)

The OIF captures PeopleSoft's approach to the enterprise and to application integration in particular. Compared to other ERP vendors, PeopleSoft has a more mature and strategic approach to interoperability. Traditionally, ERP vendors tend to view the enterprise in terms of a homogenous deployment model as far as their product suite is concerned. However, PeopleSoft has recognized the desire in many organizations for picking the best-of-breed solutions for a given category and integrating them.

Applications are typically the building blocks for an enterprise-wide integrated business solution. PeopleSoft uses the term *component* when describing application modules. In the PeopleSoft product suite, a component represents an identifiable business object, structure, or unit of work. Applications structured as components, with communication links between them, provide maximum flexibility for deploying business processes. The term *component* has many different meanings and connotations in the software paradigm. Understanding the meaning of this term within the context of PeopleSoft applications is fundamental to understanding OIF.

An example of a PeopleSoft application component would be a purchase order. Working on a component level often reveals additional integration requirements. For example, supporting centralized purchase order creation with centralized payments versus a distributed purchase order creation with centralized payments will likely have different integration requirements. These requirements are harder to identify when you're working at an application level.

Components and Integration Points

A business process can be broken down into a set of components that communicate with one another through various integration points. An integration point is defined by several functional and system attributes. Functional attributes include the following:

- **Direction of process (inbound and/or outbound)**—This attribute defines whether the integration point accepts data (inbound) or transmits data (outbound). Outbound data typically means that the component initiates communication. Inbound data means that the component accepts incoming information.
- **Application behavior**—This attribute defines the timing of the integration. Is it real-time or is it batch-oriented? And is the expected behavior one way or is a response expected?
- **Data volumes supported**—This attribute usually drives the choice of behavior. For large data volumes, you would generally choose a batch-oriented approach.

The system attributes include the following:

- **Available data formats**—This attribute defines what data format the component is capable of generating and receiving. Transformation requirements between data formats are driven by two components communicating with each other on specific integration points having different data formats.
- **Available implementation interfaces**—This attribute identifies the APIs available to programmers and applications for implementing the integration points. APIs vary from well-designed and documented objects and functions to RDBMS table structures to Flat file formats.

The PeopleSoft component structure is illustrated in Figure 11.2.

When components are tightly coupled, the two parts are linked in real-time. The called component must return some type of information before the initiating component can complete its transaction. This type of integration is sometimes referred to as *synchronous processing*, *request/reply*, or *conversation mode*.

Loosely coupled components imply that the sharing of information does not have to be immediate. The initiating component can complete its business transaction before the receiving component does anything with the shared data. This is sometimes referred to as *asynchronous processing*, *messaging*, or *publish-subscribe mode*.

I won't go into the benefits of tight coupling and loose coupling in this chapter. This subject is worthy of an entire book on its own. For the current topic, you need to know that PeopleSoft 8 supports both types of component integration. The OIF brings together PeopleSoft's broad set of application integration capabilities into a unified framework. It enables enterprises to integrate a wide range of applications and diverse business processes with PeopleSoft's enterprise application backbone.

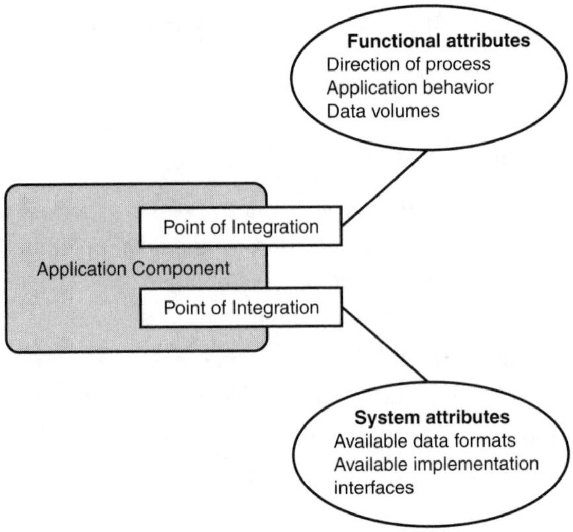
Functional attributes
Direction of process
Application behavior
Data volumes
Point of Integration
Application Component
Point of Integration
System attributes
Available data formats
Available implementation interfaces

FIGURE 11.2
PeopleSoft component structure.

Understanding PeopleSoft Application Integration Tools

Consistent with generally available solutions, most of the external focus on application integration with PeopleSoft has been in the area of tightly coupled calls into PeopleSoft. The following integration solutions are part of the tools:

- Tightly coupled inbound calls to PeopleSoft
- Tightly coupled outbound calls from PeopleSoft
- Loosely coupled inbound and outbound calls
- File-based inbound and outbound calls

PeopleTools 8 is a collection of tools introduced with the PeopleSoft Internet architecture. It includes a comprehensive messaging system for loosely coupled integration, an expanded set of tools for synchronous integration, more flexible file support, and a framework for tightly coupled outbound calls from PeopleSoft applications. Several options and technologies available in PeopleSoft 8 enable the four integration solutions in the preceding list.

Tightly Coupled Inbound Calls to PeopleSoft

Option 1: Message Agent Technology—This technology provides a high-level programmatic interface for executing PeopleSoft's application processor and is the primary tool to expose PeopleSoft transactions, allowing non-PeopleSoft systems to get data from and put data into

PeopleSoft applications. The application processor responds to the message agent calls by executing the appropriate PeopleSoft transactions. Message agent calls can be made either as C/C++ function calls or as OLE automation (COM) calls. All business rules, security, and workflow processing associated with the transaction are executed when the calls are received. The actual processing takes place on PeopleSoft's application server to maximize performance and scalability.

Option 2: Open Query API—This technology can be used to retrieve data from a PeopleSoft database by exposing a PeopleSoft query. The Open Query API consists of a high-level programmatic interface to PeopleSoft's Query tool that allows an external application to call PeopleSoft query definitions as ODBC stored procedures. When a query is called, PeopleSoft application security is invoked to validate the requesting PeopleSoft operator ID and ensure that the call returns data that the user is allowed to see. External applications can access PeopleSoft data through PeopleSoft security without having to install any PeopleSoft client software. This is possible because the Open Query API is ODBC-compliant.

Option 3: Component Interfaces—Component interfaces allow internal and external applications to invoke PeopleSoft's application business rules in a synchronous manner. External applications call methods of PeopleSoft components to achieve this. Component interfaces are exposed through a variety of language bindings, including C++, Java, COM, and XML.

Using the PeopleSoft message agent is the recommended way to access PeopleSoft components and the business logic associated with them outside the PeopleSoft online pages. It extends the reach of PeopleSoft data and business processes beyond PeopleSoft applications. The message agent allows a user to create a program that can do some of the same things that would be done in accessing the page directly. For example, a program can be written to provide the keys to a page just like an online user would do through the search dialog. The same mechanism can be used to retrieve data from the page fields, or enter data into the page fields, and save the page. The message agent performs all the same edits and security checks that an online user would use, including running any business logic associated with the page. Therefore, if the page has workflow business logic associated with it, the message agent triggers the business event.

Tightly Coupled Outbound Calls from PeopleSoft

Option 1: OLE/COM Automation—PeopleSoft has a proprietary 4GL called PeopleCode. All business rules of PeopleSoft applications are coded in PeopleCode. These PeopleCode programs can call OLE-enabled applications (automation servers) to invoke automatic processing during a PeopleSoft transaction. This mechanism is useful for integrating with external applications or third-party OLE components.

PeopleCode also allows application developers to define Windows DLL or UNIX-shared libraries as functions and to call these functions during transaction processing. In this way, PeopleCode can make calls to runtime libraries. Both of these mechanisms are useful for branching to an external component or application from within a PeopleSoft transaction.

Option 2: Business Interlink—The Business Interlink technology illustrated in Figure 11.3 is an integrated framework that allows PeopleSoft applications to access external systems in a tightly coupled mode using a standardized interface. It is essentially a plug-in framework for PeopleSoft applications capable of providing the following services:

- Querying data
- Updating data
- Adding data
- Deleting data

The services can process a single transaction in real-time, or they can process multiple transactions in a batch mode. One of the first things PeopleSoft did when building this framework was to provide a generalized interface definition that maps one-to-one to any business transaction. That generalized interface definition was called *BI Definition*. Corresponding to a BI Definition is a *BI Object*, which maps to a runtime instance of a business transaction. A BI Definition has a unique name and set of well-defined inputs and outputs. BI Objects are built using PeopleCode (Proprietary 4GL) and are essentially capable of accessing external application functionality by interfacing with appropriate plug-ins. The Business Interlink framework provides a generalized execution model for BI Objects. When a business event triggers the execution of a Business Interlink, the component processor synchronously calls the Business Interlink Processor, which, in turn, invokes the appropriate Interlink plug-in. Plug-ins can wrap different technologies and APIs such as COM, CORBA, and EJB. Access to BI Objects is enabled through language bindings such as PeopleCode binding.

Clearly, the BI Framework is a more powerful option than OLE automation because it can work with different technologies through BI plug-ins. The separation of BI Definition (meta data) from the corresponding BI Objects makes upgrades easy.

Loosely Coupled Inbound and Outbound

Option 1: Interface Tables—PeopleSoft applications use interface tables for both inbound and outbound asynchronous data exchange. Most of the interface tables are designed for importing data into PeopleSoft applications. These tables store data in SQL format, not any proprietary formats. Data is moved from the interface tables to operational data tables by executing SQL procedures provided by PeopleSoft.

Option 2: Application Messaging—The Application Messaging technology was constructed specifically to support loosely coupled inbound outbound integration. This facility allows PeopleSoft applications to publish messages during the processing of an online transaction. These messages are published in XML format and delivered to subscribing systems over a secure HTTP connection. Figure 11.4 illustrates how two components interact with each other through the application messaging facility.

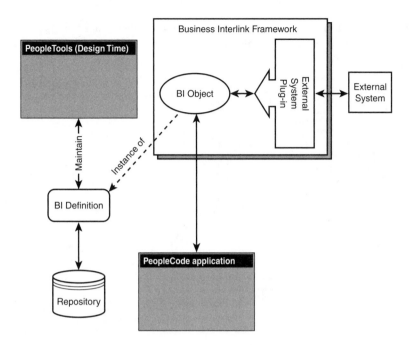

FIGURE 11.3

BI Framework components and uses.

The essence of the application messaging interaction shown in Figure 11.4 can be described in four major steps:

1. The publishing application invokes the component processor to publish a message based on a business event, which, in turn, invokes the application messaging processor.

2. The application messaging processor publishes the message as an XML document and logs a copy of the message to a message queue in the database. This process then asynchronously invokes the subscribing system's Integration Relay servlet by delivering the XML message to the subscribing system(s) over secure HTTP.

3. The subscribing Integration Relay servlet receives the XML message and invokes the application messaging processor in the subscribing system, which then logs the message in a message queue in the system's database.

4. The application messaging processor in the subscribing system asynchronously invokes the component processor to process the inbound message. The component processor then edits the message data, invokes the appropriate business rules, and updates the database.

Third-party systems can publish messages and subscribe to messages to and from the application messaging architecture over HTTP by using XML. To publish a message, the third party simply performs an HTTP post to the PeopleSoft Internet application server, passing XML documents. To subscribe to a message, the third party simply needs to be able to receive an XML message over HTTP from the PeopleSoft Internet application server.

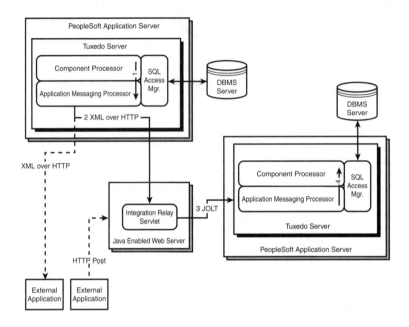

FIGURE 11.4
PeopleSoft application messaging in action.

The application messaging mechanism is the preferred mechanism for loosely coupled integration. Not only does it leverage industry standards such as HTTP and XML, but it also provides more flexibility.

File Based Inbound and Outbound

Despite the many available integration options for PeopleSoft, file based integration remains a popular and commonly deployed solution. There are a couple of reasons for its popularity. First, it is relatively easy to implement. There are none of the complexities associated with distributed computing services to contend with. Second, it is highly efficient with regard to the movement of data. The flat file inbound-outbound option is particularly applicable for batch transfers of high volume data.

With PeopleSoft version 8, a specialized application processor known as the Application Engine provides the file based integration capability. This application processor collaborates with many of the Internet Application Server services such as the Component Processor, Application Messaging, and Business Interlinks. In particular, the Application Engine uses the file I/O processing capabilities of the Component Processor to read and write files with fixed length or delimited records. It is also able to handle XML formats.

Previous versions of PeopleSoft conducted file based integration with a tool called EDI Manager. This tool enables users to map EDI messages to PeopleSoft tables and visa versa. The EDI Manager can also be used for mapping non-EDI flat files. It is possible that future versions of PeopleSoft may include a new EDI Manager enabled by the Application Engine.

Summary

This chapter described the different choices you have when seeking to integrate PeopleSoft 8 with external systems. Compared to other ERP vendors, PeopleSoft has a distinctly different view with regard to integration. The emphasis on integration is evident when you consider the integration tools and facilities available. In addition, PeopleSoft's investment in crafting the OIF extends its capabilities for integration to Web-based applications as well as legacy systems. Other vendors will undoubtedly have similar solutions in time. However, PeopleSoft has an edge when it comes to enterprise application integration (EAI) with other applications as well as in B2B integration (B2Bi).

The next chapter will cover Oracle applications. There, you will learn about the integration framework proposed by Oracle and the different interfaces available to you when considering integration with Oracle applications.

Interfacing with Oracle Applications

"For I am a bear of very little brain, and long words bother me."
—Winnie the Pooh

IN THIS CHAPTER

Although many know Oracle as simply the world's leading database vendor, the company has a strategy far broader than that. It also aims to be a leading provider of e-Business applications and all signs indicate that it is getting traction in that arena as well. Therefore, it will become increasingly important to integrate with Oracle applications as time goes on.

The primary focus of this chapter is simply to equip you with an understanding of what is required to interface with the Oracle e-Business Suite. We will discuss the various relevant topics associated with integrating external applications with Oracle e-Business suite. Although, the ideal scenario would be for Oracle to define a single method of integration interface based on industry standards, as you will discover this is not the case. This is often because of the challenges of technology innovation, the ever-expanding functionality of the applications, and the need to support customers using older versions of Oracle applications. This combination of technical and business challenges has resulted in different methods for integrating external systems with Oracle applications.

Overview of Oracle Applications

Release 11i, the latest release of Oracle Applications is given a new moniker the "Oracle e-Business Suite." This is because Oracle believes it is the first software vendor to provide a comprehensive, integrated suite of e-Business applications for the enterprise. The Oracle e-Business Suite is targeted to enable its users to leverage the new Internet business practices implemented within the applications to capitalize on the emerging new economy.

Applications in the e-Business suite are broadly divided into two categories:

- Enterprise Resource Planning (ERP) applications
- Customer Relationship Management (CRM) applications

The ERP applications suite covers almost all internal business functions/processes including Finance, Manufacturing & Supply chain, Discrete manufacturing, Process manufacturing, Order management, Procurement, Planning & scheduling, Human Resources, Projects and Strategic, Enterprise management, and Business intelligence and analysis, among others.

The CRM applications suite covers many of the customer-focused processes and functions including Marketing, Sales, Services, and Call centers. Some of the new products in the Oracle CRM 3I suite include

- Oracle Call Center Intelligence that is an internet based performance management system providing essential metrics for call-center administrators.
- Oracle Customer Case applications which is an integrated out of the box solution for running a one-stop customer-care center by collecting, analyzing, and distributing customer information throughout an enterprise.

- Other applications include iBill & Pay for billing customers and collecting payments on the internet, and Oracle Mobile Field Service which provides wireless connectivity to field-service personnel.

As opposed to companies that simply Web-enabled their application suites, Oracle was one of the first companies to see the e-commerce trend and capitalize on it as a competitive advantage. It began preparing its products for the Internet. For example in recent months, automation of Internet-based procurement is emerging as a highly effective tool for streamlining and improving the acquisition and management of goods and services. Oracle's Strategic Procurement solution provides support for automating the complete procure-to-pay cycle. It also includes some of the most mature and complete purchasing-analysis and decision support tools in the market. The solution also provides a Web-based platform to facilitate the exchange of vital business information between trading partners. The applications in the e-Business suite are designed to run on corporate Internets and the World Wide Web. The architecture of these applications is such that the procurement solution can be run as a standalone application separate from Oracle ERP. This flexibility or modularity is essential in the Internet domain where collaboration between best of breed applications is more prevalent. Oracle Strategic Procurement delivers the required support in three main areas: procurement automation, strategic sourcing, and supply-chain collaboration.

Doing business on the World Wide Web requires Internationalization of applications. With its support for globalization, Oracle e-Business suite enables its customers to have a single data center. All localization data is stored in a single code base and Unicode supports all languages.

Despite the comprehensive suite of applications from Oracle, it is highly unlikely that Oracle customers would choose to deploy the entire suite using a singular comprehensive approach. Business realities are such that a phased migration from existing legacy and other strategic applications is common practice, especially for huge projects like ERP deployments. Oracle recognizes this business need as it provides its own integration middleware Oracle Applications Interconnect (OAI) to integrate its CRM applications suite with other ERP systems.

Integrating External Systems

No ERP implementation is complete without experiencing the painful process of data conversions. One of the biggest reasons for delays of ERP implementation projects is the underestimation of data conversion tasks. Many organizations have failed in their attempts to successfully migrate to one of the ERP systems due to data conversion and migration issues.

Oracle's core competency has been in DBMS and it is not surprising to see a data-centric architecture in its e-Business applications suite. Oracle 8i is a major component of the infrastructure used by the applications. The newest release of Oracle Database Server, Oracle8i is designed for the internet platform. It integrates Oracle Application Server 4.0, Oracle interMedia (a high performance text search engine) and the ability to store and run Java and XML applications directly in a high-performance, scalable object-relational database.

As such, discussions on integration strategies for Oracle applications cannot be complete without analyzing the impact of Oracle DBMS technology. Before understanding the different methods of integrating external systems to specific points within the e-Business suite we need to identify the key integration requirements.

Generally, software vendors view their databases as strategic data repositories, resulting in the biased type of integration interfaces they provide. Most application programming interfaces (APIs) support inbound data. Oracle e-Business Suite is no exception to that. There are several methods available for moving data into the underlying Oracle databases. However, there is very little support for data extraction.

Key Integration Requirements

Some of the common integration requirements between an ERP and other systems are data-driven. There are other integration needs at a higher level (business process, business functions, etc). However, one of the drivers for the higher level integration is to minimize the complexities of data integration. The three important data integration requirements are

- Data conversion
- Data extracts
- Data synchronization

Data Conversion

Data conversion is most often a one-time effort focused on converting legacy data to a format compatible with Oracle database structures for the applications. There are exceptions where the data conversion from legacy to Oracle is required more than once as an ongoing process especially during system migration.

Regardless of the frequency, data conversion is essentially a one-way road for putting data into the Oracle applications databases. Generally, this is done as one of the first steps before deploying the applications in a production environment. The challenges of data conversion can vary but almost invariably most challenges are due to the lack of data definitions (or meta-data information).

Data in the legacy databases is typically extracted in raw format without the associated meta-data information. The data models of Oracle Applications will invariably be different from the data models of the legacy databases. Hence inserting raw data into Oracle Applications databases without checking for data integrity will result in broken business processes. Figure 12.1 depicts how data conversion occurs.

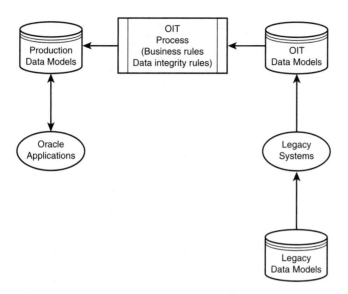

FIGURE 12.1

Data Conversion with Oracle Applications.

Oracle Applications provides a mechanism called Open Interface Tables (OIT) for preventing the corruption of the production data models and data. OIT databases are staging areas for checking data integrity of imported legacy data.

Oracle Applications use the concept of separating the production data from the inbound external applications data. This separation of data schemas (or meta-data) is useful in preserving the data integrity of the production data and at the same time supporting the need of importing data from external systems. We will discuss the role of OIT, how they enable data conversion and data synchronization in detail later in this chapter.

Data Extracts

No ERP system is an island. Not withstanding any ERP vendor's view of one central data store, in reality, there is a need for extracting data out of ERP databases. One such business pattern is the migration of operational data stored in the ERP databases to analytical databases of Business Intelligence Systems or Data warehouses.

The need for integrated data makes warehousing a necessity in most companies. One of the most common and important benefits of a well designed data warehouse is the offloading of reports and analysis from the production systems, minimizing the impact of transaction performance. A data warehouse performs the function of consolidating all kinds of operational data sources including ERP, external data, and legacy system data.

Other reasons for data extraction include parallel runs of legacy and ERP systems, collaboration between legacy and ERP systems, and data exchange between ERP and EDI trading partners.

The sheer scope of migrating existing business processes and data to a new environment is rarely a smooth, seamless event. Most organizations that have successfully implemented ERP have taken a phased approach migrating business applications by business functions. One side effect of a phased migration is the need for parallel runs of the new ERP modules and the old legacy systems to ensure a successful transition without any impact to business. One of the reasons for investing in ERP systems is to achieve significantly better business processes. Although the ERP system becomes the master source of information, frequent, regular, and scheduled data extracts are required to synchronize ERP data with legacy systems. Sometimes these legacy systems can include EDI data exchanges as well.

Oracle Applications do not have a specific interface or mechanism for supporting data extracts. Users need to build these data extracts using the underlying Oracle RDBMS table schemas and PL/SQL. PL/SQL is one of Oracle's innovations and is an extension of the standard SQL. The "PL" in PL/SQL stands for procedural language. Oracle has added procedural language capabilities on top of the standard SQL syntax. This combination of a programming language and data manipulation language is very powerful and can be used to implement complex business rules and data manipulation procedures. The downside of PL/SQL is obviously the proprietary nature of the technology. PL/SQL procedures will run only within Oracle databases.

Oracle Applications defines a number of Business Views. A Business View is a read-only database table capable of presenting a consolidated view of data from more than one database table. In some ways, the concept Business Views can be considered a mechanism for implementing data extracts. However in our opinion a proper mechanism would include tools for automating the execution of data extracts based on business/systems events, which does not exist in the Oracle Applications domain yet. Users need to develop custom PL/SQL programs to achieve this.

Data Synchronization

Data synchronization is the process of ensuring the most up-to-date state of data entities in a distributed database environment. A simple example of this would be the state of customer information in the different databases within an organization. Data synchronization is about propagating changes to the customer data in one database across all databases to ensure consistent customer information. It is often that we see master copies of data entities distributed over multiple databases. The distributed data architecture requires applications to keep the copies (slaves) of master data entities synchronized at all times. Advanced data replication tools enable us to transport and manage data between databases.

However, a bigger challenge in data synchronization is managing the differences in database schemas. This requires data transformation tools to transform raw data derived from one database schema to another database schema. There are no tools in the Oracle e-Business suite or the Oracle database to support data transformation between legacy systems and Oracle Applications databases. That responsibility is left to the external applications themselves or the EAI product used to tie the different external systems and Oracle e-Business applications.

Types of Interfaces

The latest release of Oracle applications has a much stronger integration support. Oracle has incorporated different types of interfaces to enable integration between Oracle e-Business suite and third-party products. Part of the reason for better integration support is the natural evolution of the technology. The other reason is the growing realization that generally customers prefer best of breed solutions rather than "put all eggs in one basket" solutions, so to speak.

The almost innumerable modules of Oracle e-Business Suite use one or more of the following interfaces for integrating with external systems or integration between modules:

- Open Interface Tables (OIT) and Business Views (both of these are based on Oracle tables).
- ASCII files upload and download with Oracle's SQL Loader—This is the most rudimentary mechanism for data integration. The difference between ASCII files and OIT interface upload is that the PL/SQL procedures which encapsulate business rules and data integrity rules work with OIT schemas.
- Electronic Data Exchange (EDI)—EDI is the traditional mechanism for supply chain integration. Oracle supports EDI transactions in specific integration scenarios.
- XML.

In addition, an XML layer is available above the OIT and PL/SQL interfaces that makes it possible to receive results and produce Oracle data in XML format. This layer also provides utilities to map the XML to and from formats required by existing interfaces. However the current XML support is largely focused on supply chains and supporting Oracle exchanges (B2B exchanges).

With the emphasis on Internet enabled applications and enabling Internet business practices, Oracle e-Business interface types can be broadly classified as follows:

- Interfaces for integrating demand-side e-Business applications. Demand-side applications include customer collaboration systems, online stores, self-service Web sires, interaction centers for customer care, and mobile hand-held devices. Oracle CRM applications are largely focused on automating and managing the demands of migrating front office operations to the Internet. The OAI integration scheme is useful in integrating Oracle CRM with older versions of Oracle ERP and SAP/R3.
- Interfaces for integrating supply-side e-Business applications such as Order management and supply chain management. EDI and XML integration is useful in this domain.

Understanding OIT

An OIT (Open Interface Table) is a public table exposed by the Oracle ERP applications suite. Oracle recommends that these tables be used for data integration since they are de-coupled from the actual production data tables. Updating the OIT with external data does not directly impact the production data tables.

Oracle provides PL/SQL procedures for moving the OIT data to production tables. These procedures implement business rules and data integrity rules required to ensure the data entering the production tables would not disrupt the operations. The PL/SQL procedures are not triggered automatically and need to be invoked from outside.

The OIT mechanism is essentially a batch interface useful for uploading high volume data. OIT mechanism is not optimized for inserting data into Oracle applications in an online format.

Error Handling with OIT

The two levels of error handling procedures that OIT users need to handle are

- PL/SQL errors resulting from failures during data upload (SQL inserts) and during execution of the PL/SQL procedure
- Errors resulting due to the uploaded data not complying with the business rules and data integrity rules implemented by the PL/SQL procedures

The first level of error handling can be considered as system level error handling and is likely to be encountered due to misspelled procedure names or insufficient permissions. The second level of error handling can be considered as business/application level error handling and is likely to be encountered due to mismatch between OIT schemas and the raw data from external applications. Handling data level errors in a batch mode can result in a negative impact on the business since any error recovery procedures required may not be executed in a timely manner.

OIT Execution Flow

The OIT execution flow is composed of the following sequential tasks:

1. Loading (Insert) data into the specific OIT.
2. Invoking the appropriate PL/SQL process or processes.
3. Checking for any resulting data error.
4. Executing recovery actions.

The four step sequential process is shown in Figure 12.2.

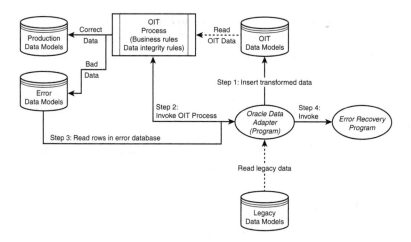

FIGURE 12.2

OIT integration process flow.

The diagram above shows an example program named "Oracle Data Adapter" executing the process of reading the legacy data and transforming it to match the specific OIT interface schema before inserting the transformed data into the OIT database. This is the first step; once all the legacy data is inserted into the OIT database the adapter program should invoke the appropriate OIT processes and execute them. This will result in the PL/SQL based OIT processes to update the production databases with valid data and insert all invalid data to specific tables within the Oracle Applications databases designed to store invalid data. Once the OIT processes have completed their tasks, the adapter program needs to check the error tables for invalid data before invoking the error recovery programs.

The architecture of the adapter program can be simple or complex depending on the computing environments. The basic tasks however remain the same.

Understanding EDI and XML Interfaces

Oracle also supports EDI and XML based interface for integrating supply-side applications in the e-Business applications suite, specifically the Order Management modules. EDI has been a standard for exchanging data between organizations (also referred to as trading partners) for a long time.

Traditionally EDI solutions have been deployed as private exchanges driven by buyers. XML based B2B exchange platforms as Oracle Exchange enables public exchanges where the trading partnerships are more dynamic.

Oracle's EDI Gateway enables Oracle Applications to communicate electronically between trading partners by using standard EDI transaction sets. The Oracle EDI modules interface with any EDI translator, and are tightly integrated with the Oracle Applications suite, including Oracle's self-service Web Applications, to provide high-volume back-end transaction processing.

For example, a supplier can send a customer the latest price/sales catalog information via electronic data interchange (EDI). This information can then be imported into the catalog information, directly into Oracle Purchasing as blanket purchase agreements or as catalog quotations, depending on which you choose. EDI also automatically updates the item master in Oracle Inventory and applies sourcing rules to the imported item information in Oracle Purchasing.

Understanding OAI

Oracle Applications InterConnect (OAI) is a robust and flexible applications integration platform that enables integration of Oracle CRM suite of applications with ERP solutions such as SAP R/3, Oracle Applications release 10.7, and some legacy systems.

OAI is designed to facilitate the integration of Oracle CRM and enterprise applications with integration tools and preconfigured integrations for some ERP systems like SAP/R3. The OAI solution includes iStudio, an easy-to-use wizard-based integration specification tool, enabling its users to visually review, modify, and make the changes necessary to tailor the pre-packaged integration to match users business needs. OAI is built upon proven Oracle server and database technologies and takes full advantage of their features and functionality. The messaging backbone for OAI is supported via the Advanced Queuing features of Oracle 8i.

The primary objective of OAI is to provide an easy, business oriented mechanism for defining the business processes integrating CRM (front office) functionality to ERP (back office functionality). Oracle e-Business suite includes a prepackaged Oracle CRM–SAP/R3 interface. Similar interfaces to other ERP systems can be built using OAI technology.

Assessing the Oracle Applications Interfaces

You've been introduced to the three primary integration interfaces employed by the Oracle e-Business suite—OIT, XML/EDI, and OAI. Each interface addresses a particular type of integration. Figure 12.3 depicts the role of the OIT, XML/EDI, and OAI interfaces in the Oracle Applications integration architecture.

The OIT and EDI/XML interfaces are externally oriented, in that they are used to move data between Oracle modules to external systems. The OIT is used primarily for integrating with legacy systems, commonplace in EAI. It is based on externalization of Oracle tables and is simplistic in concept. The EDI/XML interface gateway enables the deployment of the B2Bi data exchange pattern (covered in Chapter 3, "e-Business Integration Patterns"). Native data is converted into EDI or XML and transmitted through the gateway mechanism.

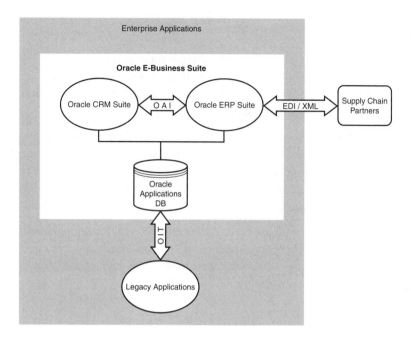

FIGURE 12.3

Oracle e-Business Suite Interface Types.

In the Oracle Applications integration architecture, OAI is internally focused. The OAI links the CRM modules with ERP modules. It utilizes the Oracle database message queuing mechanism for integration within the Oracle e-Business suite.

Oracle Applications interfaces appear to be far easier to grasp and apply than those of SAP. However, their simplicity is founded on a database-centric approach, unlike the more complex APIs available in SAP. Mechanisms such as OIT and OAI use facilities linked to the Oracle database. This makes for easier deployment but limited capability. In particular, the OIT mechanism provides no support for near real-time exchange of data. The focus on data exchange approach is indicative of the database roots of the Oracle Applications offering. The OIT works well for a one-time data conversion typical for database migration scenarios. However, the OIT becomes a serious limitation for a dynamic, real-time integration of data. In environments such as financial markets or B2B trading, where up-to-date information is critical, this latency of integrated data can be costly.

What is required from Oracle Applications is an object-based RFC type programmatic interface. The BAPI interface in SAP is a prime example of where Oracle should be heading with its interfaces.

Summary

The Oracle e-Business suite is a very large set of applications and technologies. It is also a very powerful system capable of enabling its users to transition into the new economy. However, the path to success is riddled with typical implementation and integration issues such as data conversion and data synchronization.

Oracle applications have evolved to include better integration support. However most of the integration components are targeted to enable integration between Oracle CRM and other ERP packages, or are focused on enabling internal Oracle applications integration. There is very little support for legacy system integration except the traditional OIT mechanism. XML and EDI transactions can be used as alternative techniques for integration with supply chain partners.

The bottom line is integration with external systems requires additional programming work and Oracle e-Business suite is no exception. The trend however is clearly towards more standards based API for enabling faster and better integration with legacy and other external applications.

Interfacing with Siebel eBusiness 2000

"To suppose that the eye with all its inimitable contrivances for adjusting the focus to different distances, for admitting different amounts of light, and for the correction of spherical and chromatic aberration, could have been formed by natural selection, seems, I confess, absurd in the highest degree."
—Charles Darwin (The Origin of Species, London: John Murray, 1859)

IN THIS CHAPTER

This chapter will discuss integration with Siebel, the leading customer relationship management (CRM) application. The last couple of years have witnessed a phenomenal growth in the CRM application space. The inevitable shift to e-Business has forced organizations to focus more on the demand chain—that is, customer relationship management. This change has marked a shift of emphasis from enterprise resource planning (ERP) back office systems to CRM front office applications. CRM package applications such as Siebel gained in prominence, resulting in the ERP vendors scrambling to build CRM solutions of their own to stay in the race. This chapter will provide an overview of Siebel's latest offering—Siebel eBusiness 2000—and discuss in detail the available mechanisms to interface with Siebel.

Overview of Siebel 2000

Traditional CRM applications were expected to help sales, marketing, and service-oriented business processes. However, the Internet has changed this application space as well. Indeed, the impact of the Internet on CRM applications is both profound and visible. Even before the advent of e-Business, the sales process was a multichannel process. Organizations have used several different methods or channels to access and keep their customers for some time. The Internet has become yet another channel; in the view of some, it is the ultimate channel for engaging and managing customers.

Because the focus of this chapter is indeed Siebel applications, I won't discuss the CRM technology space in general. An entire book could be written on this subject and the challenges of implementing a successful CRM strategy. It is evident that Siebel itself has seen huge changes in its implementations and product offerings. Like most application vendors, Siebel has affixed the now familiar *e-Business* tag to the Siebel product line. The latest version of Siebel, known as Siebel eBusiness 2000, warrants a closer look, especially in light of what it takes to integrate with other enterprise systems.

Siebel eBusiness 2000 is the only solution that enables organizations to manage, synchronize, and coordinate sales, marketing, and customer service across all communication channels and points of customer contact. The channels supported include the Web, the call center, field sales, services, and reseller channels. In some ways, the Siebel product is unique in its capabilities to integrate with other systems. Much of an application integration capability is driven by its internal architecture. Inasmuch as the application integration architecture is open and has support for industry standards, it is better positioned as an effective solution.

With a wide variety of integration technologies based on more than one standard, choosing the right interface is not an easy task. Before this chapter delves deeper into the different mechanisms of integration with Siebel, you need to take some time to understand the Siebel application architecture. This will lead you into better understanding the reasoning for the integration strategies proposed in this chapter.

Siebel Application Architecture

In its enterprise application integration (EAI) strategy, Siebel claims that it is committed to providing an open architecture that enables customers and partners to seamlessly integrate Siebel data and processes with non-Siebel data and processes. To that effect, the Siebel application architecture can be defined at a high level as having three distinct layers:

- User Interface
- Object Manager
- Data Manager

User Interface Layer

The user interface layer holds all the screens of Siebel applications. These screens are ActiveX controls and OLE2-compliant objects. Therefore, other applications besides Siebel can integrate with Siebel using industry standards. ActiveX and OLE2 can be considered industry standards in the desktop space.

Siebel user interfaces or screens are developed in a proprietary language called Siebel VB. To Siebel's credit, the company has provided users with Siebel VB tools (the Siebel VB Editor, Compiler, and Debugger). It is very rare that product vendors support proprietary scripting languages with a broad set of tools.

Object Manager Layer

The object manager layer is the middle layer, holding the business logic encapsulated in business objects and components. The Siebel Business Object interfaces make up a collection of objects that expose Siebel data and functionality to external routines (including user interfaces), which are written in Siebel VB or other languages external to the Siebel application. The Siebel Business Object interfaces are OLE2-compliant, thus enabling integration of other OLE2-based applications.

Data Manager Layer

Siebel applications use RDBMS technology to store persistent objects. Not surprisingly, there is a paradigm mismatch between the business logic and state encapsulated as objects and the RDBMS databases that store data in rows and columns. The data manager layer handles these mismatches and converts objects into RDBMS table rows and vice versa. The data manager layer is not exposed to the external world; it is used by the object manager layer as a mechanism for storing and retrieving business object data and state information.

As you will note from Figure 13.1, the clear separation of each layer is the strength of Siebel application architecture. Usage of industry standards-based interfaces to some of the layers further simplifies any integration requirement.

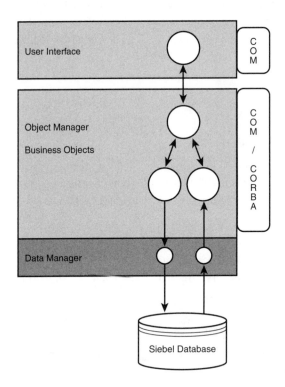

FIGURE 13.1
Siebel application architecture.

Both the user interface layer and object manager layer have standards-based interfaces that expose selected objects within each layer. The user interface objects are exposed using COM interfaces. The fact that COM is available only on the Windows platform may seem like a limitation. However, most user desktops are Windows-based. This is especially true with packaged-applications users as well as Internet end users. The business objects inside the object manager layer are exposed using COM and CORBA interfaces. The use of CORBA Interface Definition Language (IDL) enables third-party applications running on non-Windows platforms to access Siebel business objects.

There are no interfaces to the Siebel database. This is intentional, and the reason is to prevent applications from bypassing the Siebel business logic, which processes the data. A mechanism in the Siebel EAI tools enables mass data uploads and downloads to Siebel databases.

These capabilities may be required to ensure data synchronization. The COM and CORBA interfaces provided by Siebel have bidirectional integration capabilities or interfaces. This architecture has proven to be a strong asset, especially in the definition of the EAI solution for Siebel. The EAI choices in Siebel will be discussed later in this chapter. For now, let me say that Siebel does deserve compliments for enforcing an open architecture for its applications.

Understanding Siebel Thin Client Products

As you learned earlier, CRM applications always support multiple channels of access to ensure their users can invoke the applications from various mediums. This requirement is an ideal case for developing thin client products, which have a minimum of three layers or tiers. The user interface layer is a very thin layer that consists of only the application user interfaces. Siebel offers the following three types of thin client products:

- Thin Client for Windows
- Java thin client
- HTML thin client

You might be thinking about the relevance of discussing these thin client technologies from an integration perspective. However, if you understand that these three products target three different user access mediums (Windows desktop, platform-independent Java clients, and Web browsers), then understanding the technologies and their capabilities for integration is beneficial.

The benefit of thin client architecture is the added flexibility it provides in distribution of the business logic and data stores from the user interfaces. Deploying the thin client technologies enables Siebel users to integrate their legacy systems at a business logic level rather then being constrained to integrate at only the data store level. The following sections will provide a brief overview of the thin client technologies of Siebel. This information will prove useful in your understanding the EAI capabilities of Siebel, which will be described next.

Thin Client for Windows

Since its inception a few years ago, the Web browser has come a long way. Today it is one of the most preferred platforms for thin client applications on Windows platforms. Siebel supports two mechanisms for thin clients on Windows, namely the ActiveX thin client for Internet Explorer 4.x or higher and Netscape plug-in for Netscape Navigator 4.x or higher.

The ActiveX thin client has two parts: ActiveX application control, which essentially provides the user interface, and ActiveX data control, which wraps Siebel data as COM objects. The benefit of the ActiveX strategy is obvious to anyone who has used Visual Basic (VB) to build applications.

The ActiveX application controls can be embedded in a VB form. All the UI-Context methods are available, enabling Siebel users to build VB applications, which can integrate with legacy data on one user interface. Third-party COM components can be easily mixed with Siebel ActiveX controls to build highly customized and integrated Siebel applications. Siebel client applications are built using Siebel VB (a Microsoft VB-compliant application environment).

Java Thin Client

Although the Windows platform has the most market share in the client desktop space, the Web browser has become the default platform for e-Business applications. You have two choices for building Web applications: HTML and Java applets. I'll discuss Java thin clients first because Java is a far more powerful environment and continues to evolve.

Siebel has a Java thin client application (not a Java applet) for non-Windows operating systems. Currently, only SUN Solaris 2.6 is supported (or tested, as is the case with Java technology). Before starting the Java application, you need to modify a configuration file (Siebel.cfg) located on the same machine as the application to point to the correct Siebel servers (Object Manager).

Java applications run on a multitude of platforms (any platform capable of hosting a Java Virtual Machine, or JVM). To be really scalable and portable, the Siebel Object Manager also has similar capabilities. COM interfaces are limited to the Windows platform. Here, CORBA steps up to the task of being platform independent. What the Java thin client achieves in terms of multiple platform support for the user interface, CORBA achieves for business objects and the Siebel Object Manager. The Siebel CORBA Object Manager is a CORBA/IIOP-compliant server that has the same functionality as the Siebel Object Manager, which runs on the Windows platform.

HTML Thin Client

The thinnest of all thin client technologies is the HTML client. The Web browser in its role as an HTML container does the bulk of the work of interpreting HTML tags and generating the user interface. HTML is just a definition of the actual interface and, as such, is very lightweight. At the same time, it is also limited in its capabilities.

The Siebel HTML thin client is deployed for the eBusiness applications eService, eChannel, and eSales within the Siebel 2000 application suite. The HTML thin client is a cross-platform, browser-independent client that extends the Siebel Enterprise Application to the Web as shown in Figure 13.2. Transformation of Siebel data accessed via Siebel business objects to HTML tags is the job of the Siebel Web Engine (SWE). The SWE is essentially made up of Siebel extensions to the Microsoft Web server, Microsoft Internet Information Server 4.0. The SWE is also responsible for communicating with the appropriate Siebel Object Manager hosting the business objects.

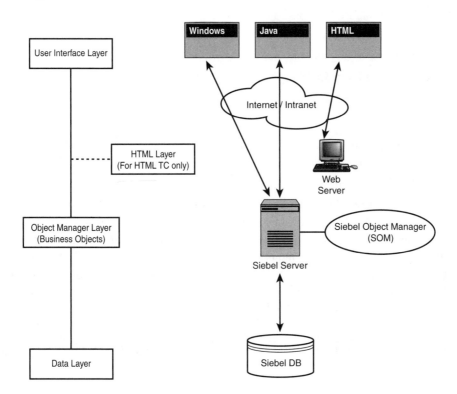

13

INTERFACING WITH
SIEBEL EBUSINESS
2000

FIGURE 13.2

Siebel thin client architecture and products.

The real benefits of the thin client architecture and products are realized when integrating external applications and interfacing with different technologies. That is the focus of the next section in this chapter.

Siebel Application Integration Strategy

Siebel has one of the strongest AI strategies in the packaged software market today, which is captured in the Siebel Integration Solutions Suite. At the heart of the Integration Solutions is a product called Enterprise Integration Manager (EIM). Its primary objective is to support asynchronous data exchange, especially of large data volumes. The other important component is the Siebel Object Interfaces, which support real-time inter-application integration. Siebel also supports third-party messaging and middleware. To further simplify integration among Siebel and other popular ERP systems, Siebel provides out-of-the-box interfaces to SAP R/3, JD Edwards, Oracle, Broadvision, Ariba, and so on. Siebel EAI is a suite of modules consisting of the following:

- Siebel connectors
- Third-party messaging and middleware
- Enterprise Integration Manager
- Business object interfaces
- ActiveX plug-ins

You already know the role of ActiveX controls or plug-ins. This section will take a closer look at some of the other modules. Before you get further into the modules, you need to understand some of the integration requirements:

Bulk movement of data—This can involve moving large quantities of data between Siebel and other applications (for example, sharing customer and material master data).

Real-time interaction—This includes activities such as initiating transactions and retrieving data for display or modification, typically at the record- and event-driven level.

Unified and consistent view of data—In addition to the preceding requirements, the EAI modules should be adaptable to changes (business, technology) and be easily implemented, customized, and upgraded.

Understanding the Enterprise Integration Manager (EIM)

The Enterprise Integration Manager module provides data exchange services, including importing data from RDBMS tables of other applications. Apart from importing data, the EIM provides other services such as updating Siebel data, deleting Siebel data, exporting Siebel data to external applications, and merging data. This comprehensive set of services ensures a synchronized database. The EIM module handles multiple data sources and types. Users have full control over exact tables and columns to be processed. To maintain the data integrity of the Siebel data store, Siebel provides a set of interface tables. EIM interfaces with these interface tables and converts data between Siebel base tables (production data) and the interface tables. This is illustrated in Figure 13.3 below.

To see how the EIM module is used, consider a real-world example. Siebel has a SAP R/3 connector. The definitions of the mappings between the two applications (Siebel and SAP) reside in Siebel tools; the runtime execution of these maps is controlled by a new server component called the Siebel Enterprise Interface Scheduler. At runtime, the Enterprise Interface Scheduler collects IDocs generated by SAP and performs the necessary data transformations and delivery to Siebel Interface tables. In Figure 13.3, the Enterprise Interface Scheduler is one of the Custom Subscriber processes. The Enterprise Interface Scheduler then invokes EIM, which delivers this data to the base tables. Several instances of the Enterprise Interface Scheduler may be run concurrently. This process can also occur in the reverse direction, from Siebel to SAP.

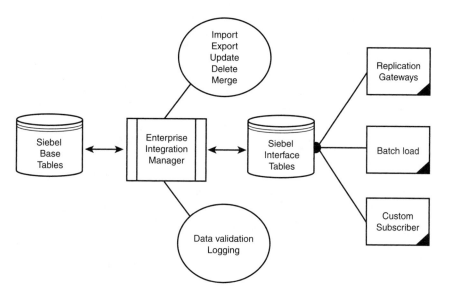

FIGURE 13.3
The role of the Enterprise Integration Manager (EIM).

Understanding the Business Integration Manager

Although the EIM module is useful for data synchronization, it is still a batch-oriented interface. For achieving real-time integration, Siebel built a suite of modules packaged as the Business Integration Manager. Its primary components include integration object technology, business services, and adapters. The role of an integration object is to marshal data between adapters or connectors and the Siebel business objects. Siebel business objects encapsulate the business logic of Siebel applications. Siebel adapters provide connectivity and data exchange services to third-party applications. The missing link between the adapters and business objects is an integration object.

To simplify building these integration objects, Siebel provides an Integration Object Wizard, which generates the integration objects. An integration object exposes the internal structure of Siebel business objects and effectively encapsulates the business object from external data as shown in Figure 13.4. Data transformation and mapping between two integration objects are handled by Siebel business services. These services can be built using Siebel VB (on the Windows platform) and Siebel eScript (on non-Windows platforms) scripting languages. Siebel adapters have similar capabilities but are targeted at data transformation and mapping between external applications and integration objects.

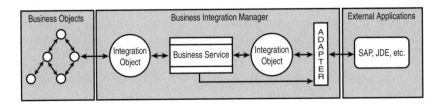

FIGURE 13.4

The Siebel Business Integration Manager.

The combination of integration objects, business services, and adapters enables Siebel to quickly integrate with third-party applications. The Business Integration Manager is the infrastructure for out-of-the-box integration between Siebel and SAP R/3. Business services map equivalent entities in Siebel (Account, Contact, Product, and Order) and SAP (Customer, Material, and Order). The SAP adapter is responsible for interacting with SAP BAPI and IDoc interfaces, whereas the integration objects tie these components together.

Summary

This chapter covered the most important aspects of Siebel integration. This Siebel packaged application is unique because of its comprehensive application integration solution. These EAI modules are based on two primary standards, COM and CORBA, and ensure a unified view of data across applications. The three-tier application architecture is adaptable to change (business and technology) and is easy to configure and maintain. Figure 13.5 illustrates Siebel's support of integration at three levels: applications, business objects, and data.

With an open architecture, supporting tools, and standards-based integration solutions, Siebel is on the right track to succeed in the e-Business market, where integration is a fundamental requirement.

Having covered the popular application packages, I will discuss how to interface with legacy mainframe systems in the next chapter. Rather than doing away with mainframe systems altogether, many organizations are realizing the need for package applications to coexist with legacy systems. This should make the next chapter important reading for any integration specialist.

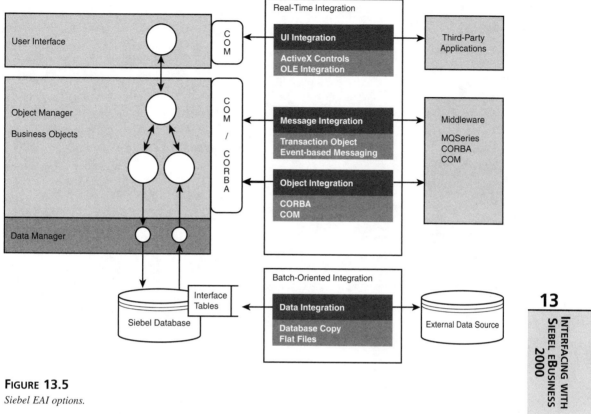

FIGURE 13.5

Siebel EAI options.

Interfacing with Legacy Applications

"R2D2, you know better than to trust a strange computer."
—C3PO in Episode V: The Empire Strikes Back

IN THIS CHAPTER

Even today, many Fortune 500 companies still run business-critical applications on mainframe computers. And despite the move to package applications, most of them are older COBOL applications. This fact may sound surprising if you cut your teeth with C, C++, and Java running on UNIX and Windows platforms. However, in the last decade, the promised newer technologies slated as replacements for COBOL mainframe applications simply haven't materialized. The list of proposed successors to the mainframe applications include the Open Systems initiative with UNIX; relational databases and SQL, CORBA, C++, and Microsoft Windows, all of which were supposed to quickly lead to the demise of the mainframe. Although each aforementioned technology is successful in its own right, it didn't replace the mainframe but rather has augmented the enterprise environment with more platforms and varied applications. In short, these older business-critical mainframe applications haven't disappeared. Instead, their enduring nature inspired the phrase *legacy applications* as an industry moniker for mainframe-based applications. Other terms such as *heritage systems* attempt to indicate the age of some of the technologies without minimizing the business value of these applications. This chapter will discuss the different types of legacy applications and the various means of integration available.

Why Have These Systems Endured?

These legacy systems have proven to be enduring and extremely resistant to displacement for three primary reasons:

- Displacement of legacy systems is costly.
- Displacement of legacy systems is risky.
- Distributed client/server systems still don't measure up.

Displacement of Legacy Systems Is Costly

Systems are generally not replaced because of technology innovations alone, nor should they be. A ratified return on investment (ROI) model is always a prerequisite before major investment initiatives are undertaken. Upon strict analysis, such initiatives are difficult to implement and often cost prohibitive. As the cost of mainframe processing power measured in million instructions per second(MIPS), has come down and the total cost of client/server systems is fully accounted for, it becomes increasingly difficult to displace legacy systems from an ROI perspective.

Displacement of Legacy Systems Is Risky

The risky nature of displacing legacy systems falls under the "if it ain't broke, don't fix it" axiom. Replacing systems that have run the business reliably for years and possibly even decades is a high-risk proposition. Legacy enterprise systems are valuable not only for the enterprise data accumulated over many years, but also for the debugged business logic that has been proven through the test of time and use. Many CIOs prefer the path of least resistance rather than undertaking unnecessary change. In recent years, conventional wisdom is to eschew reengineering applications in favor of integration of these applications with other enterprise data resources.

Distributed Client/Server Systems Still Don't Measure Up

The notion that distributed client/server systems are not adequate sounds a little harsh, but distributed systems are only now approaching the kind of reliability that you have come to expect from mainframe applications. Many UNIX hardware vendors are getting to the four-nines level of reliability; that is, the system will stay up 99.99% of time. Mainframe systems have been there for years. Furthermore, mainframe-based storage technology is simply more mature than its distributed systems counterparts.

This statement may be affirming the obvious, but IBM has been a leader in the mainframe systems arena ever since introducing the technology in the 1960s. A few other companies, such as Amdahl, Hitachi, and Fujitsu, are offering competing mainframe computing environments. However, IBM is still the driving force in this market and will likely remain so. Therefore, the discussions around mainframe integration will revolve around IBM offerings. This chapter will also discuss certain new technologies from IBM to enable mainframe integration with the Web and other e-Business systems.

Types of Mainframe Application Integration

A recurring problem faced with older applications is the lack of enough resources able to modify or extend the applications. The Y2K problem highlighted the issues of modifying legacy applications for business logic linked to a date format. Modifying legacy applications for e-Business would likely prove even more costly. This makes defining nonintrusive methods for mainframe application integration vitally important. Nonintrusive methods at different levels, both data and business logic, will enable integration without resulting in changes to the application code.

An essential component of any nonintrusive integration method is an appropriate API. Without an API providing access to existing functionality and data, you would likely have to modify the target application code. Before you get into the details of some of the available APIs for integrating mainframe applications, a quick analysis of the mainframe technology space is useful. Some of the important components of IBM mainframe technology space are shown in Figure 14.1.

This figure is by no means a complete picture of IBM mainframe technologies, but it provides a snapshot of important technologies. Numerous other system and application technologies are not shown. Application integration in the IBM mainframe domain is complex, which makes a generic integration approach extremely difficult and almost impossible to define. There are multiple operating systems, numerous databases, and different network protocols. For instance, integration at the data level may involve variations of mainframe database technologies such as DB2, IMS, VSAM, and ADABAS. Each technology is markedly different:

- DB2 is IBM's mainframe RDBMS and is often the default relational database for the mainframe, not unlike Oracle appears to be on UNIX.
- IMS comes in two flavors: IMS-TM (transaction manager) and IMS-DB (database management system).

- VSAM is the Virtual Sequential Access Manager. It provides access to indexed files and is still widely used in many mainframe applications despite the success of DB2.
- ADABAS is Software AG's hierarchical database. It is noted for its high performance capability.

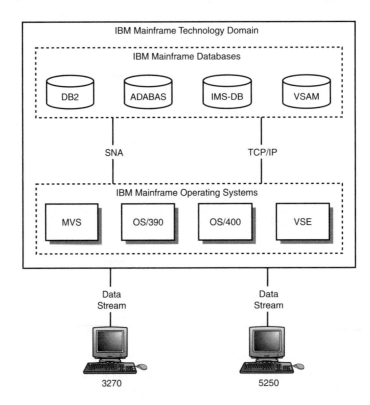

FIGURE 14.1

IBM Mainframe Technology Domain.

Mainframes also have their own system-dependent displays and peripheral devices such as printers. These display terminals generally require a controller to provide most of their functionality and the required physical connectivity between the display and the host. These display units form the only user interface between mainframe applications and their end users. As the mainstream IT moved away from host-based computing to client/server computing, users found the IBM system terminals a limiting proposition.

The desktop PC era brought powerful computers to the end users' desks. A cheaper alternative to the system terminals was required. Terminal emulation software was a direct result of this need. The primary function of terminal emulation software is to replace the costly terminal hardware with software capable of providing similar functions on cheaper PCs, as shown in Figure 14.2.

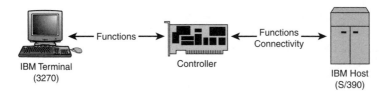

FIGURE 14.2

An example of system-dependent terminals.

This figure shows an IBM 3270 terminal connected to an S/390 type of host. The controller provides the physical connectivity and functions to access and interact with the applications on the host machine.

This terminal emulation technology has particular applicability in the integration world. Despite being monolithic from an architectural perspective, the variation of operating systems and technologies on the mainframe makes it difficult to uncover a general mechanism for integration. Terminal emulation is actually the closest generalized approach available, so the following section explores it in some detail.

Understanding IBM Terminal Emulation

As the name suggests, terminal emulation is a piece of technology capable of emulating a terminal display or controller. Any discussion of terminal emulation primarily revolves around IBM 3270 and IBM 5250 emulation technologies. The 3270 displays use the IBM-defined 3270 data stream to interact with applications on S/390 hosts. Similarly, the 5250 displays use the 5250 data stream to interact with applications on AS/400 and S/3x hosts. The data streams, as depicted in Figure 14.3, support both functional handling (such as screen handling and session management) and connectivity between the hosts and emulation software.

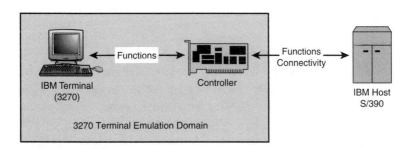

FIGURE 14.3

Terminal emulation domain.

This figure shows that terminal emulation software replaces the actual IBM terminal as well as the controller. The features and functions of these two components need to be emulated in a software environment. This can be achieved in part because, even with the original hardware environment, the functions are possible because of the data stream transported back and forth between the host and the terminal. Controlling the transport of data is the job of specific Logical Unit (LU) sessions for screen and keyboard handling, printing, file transfers, and so on. The basic features of terminal emulation programs will be covered later. But before you get to that topic, take some time to explore the structure of the data stream.

Structure of Data Stream

The focal point of the emulation software is the data streams used for interacting between the peripheral devices and applications. The data stream depicted in Figure 14.4 is a two-tiered structure made up of a base data stream and an extension data stream. The base data stream provides the functionality required for basic user-application interactions, including screen definitions, differentiation between literal and data fields, and so on. The extension data stream (commonly called *extended data stream*) provides additional capabilities for expressing color, additional character sets (single and double-byte character sets), extended highlighting (blinking and so on) and field validation (validation of data within a field).

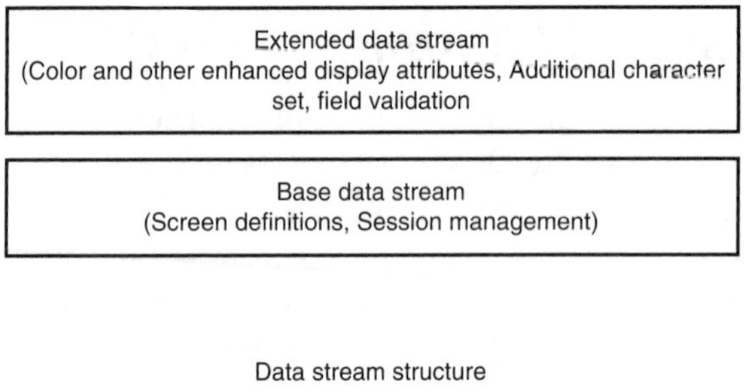

```
┌────────────────────────────────────────────────────────┐
│              Extended data stream                        │
│ (Color and other enhanced display attributes, Additional character │
│              set, field validation)                      │
└────────────────────────────────────────────────────────┘
┌────────────────────────────────────────────────────────┐
│                Base data stream                          │
│       (Screen definitions, Session management)           │
└────────────────────────────────────────────────────────┘
```

Data stream structure

Figure 14.4
Two tiers of the data stream.

Not all emulation software supports all the features of the extended data stream. This could be a problem, especially when users would expect the host-based mainframe applications to run unchanged after replacing the IBM terminals with emulation software. This problem is solved by the host computer's capability to query the terminals and emulation software about their data stream features.

Basic Features of Terminal Emulation

Typically, terminal emulation software does a lot more than just emulate display. Generally, emulation software also supports local and network printing, transferring files between the host and PC computers, as well as having an API or some sort of scripting capability for automating execution of repetitive tasks.

Display Emulation

Display emulation is the emulation of the presentation space, keyboard operation, and host program interaction of legacy fixed-function displays. Traditionally, these displays were attached to a control unit of some type (for example, an IBM 3x74 or 5x94) that provided the connection to the host system and shared in the processing of keystrokes and host data streams.

Printing

Over the years, printing has moved away from large systems to workstations. Printing can be divided into screen-printing and file printing. Depending on the emulation program, both screen-printing and file-printing jobs can be sent to the printer directly attached to the workstation or redirected to a LAN printer. Alternatively, the printing can also be done on an enterprise system printer.

File Transfer

File transfer is the capability to move files between the host and PC. This capability has long been a requirement for products in a networked environment. The whole idea of replacing terminal with software emulation programs is to move from a host-based environment to a LAN-based environment. The better emulation products have faster file transfer features and support more formats as well.

API (Application Programming Interface)

Terminal emulation software gives end users more flexibility partly because of the other applications that can be accessed from the same PC. This capability generally gives rise to the requirement of moving data between screens and applications on the PC. The higher-end emulation programs also have a rich set of API and/or scripting capabilities, which are helpful in customizing the presentation and interaction of host data. They are also helpful in automating and scheduling repetitive and time-consuming tasks.

All the features described here enable mainframe application users to use PCs instead of IBM terminals. Using terminal emulation software to facilitate mainframe integration requires a few other fundamental features, which will be discussed next.

Role of Terminal Emulation in e-Business Integration

The concepts of terminal emulation can definitely enable nonintrusive integration of mainframe applications but not without additional features to handle the resulting challenges. The typical terminal emulation software deals with connectivity, recognition of the data streams, rendering the screens for the end users, and handling user interactions. Application integration is much more complex because it does not involve end users interacting with the mainframe applications. The perceptions and decisions made by end users at runtime are absent during automation of transactions in e-Business Integration. In addition, an integration flow tends to be much broader in scope compared to simply navigating multiple application screens.

The introduction of an intelligent screen flow management component is needed to enable automatic terminal-emulated participation of mainframe applications in the integration flow. Integrating at the application level via terminal emulation provides the benefit of having the interaction conducted through the application logic. This means nothing will be allowed that isn't normally permitted by an end user. However, the following complexities are involved in setting up the flows using the emulation software:

- Screen identification
- Flow management
- Session management
- Exception management

Screen Identification

A common problem with terminal emulation is screen identification. It is a problem because many screen designs and layouts appear similar despite actually enacting different actions such as Add, Delete, and Change. Although end users have the capacity to identify the appropriate screen based on the selected action, the challenge is to provide an equivalent capability for the automated integration environment. Providing this capability is easier said than done, especially when legacy applications haven't been designed with future integration in scope.

Often automated screen identification is accomplished by providing a knowledge-base facility. This knowledge base stores unique identifying characteristics of screens, enabling automatic runtime identification and validation at the appropriate time. Also, emulation software capable of supporting the extended data streams is better suited to solve screen identification problems because screens can be uniquely identified by encoding captured within an extended data stream.

Flow Management

One of the biggest challenges of using unchanged mainframe applications and terminal emulation techniques for integration is managing the underlying flow of screens and the resulting user navigation. Because the flow of screens cannot be altered, the burden of dealing with the navigation falls on the emulation software.

Generally, the demands of the e-Business Integration flow require multiple sessions with varied actions. At times, it may involve multiple legacy systems as well. For example, a simple transaction of adding a new banking customer may result in multiple sessions over three different legacy applications, as in the following scenario:

- **Session #1**—Adding customer information to a Customer Management database
- **Session #2**—Performing credit checks with a gateway application that interfaces with an external credit checking facility
- **Session #3**—Opening a new account for the customer in an Account Management program

All three sessions may correspond to a single e-Business Integration flow. Hence, the capability to define, capture, and execute a complex flow involving multiple legacy applications, potentially different actions, and involving several screens is a requirement for emulation software in the integration domain.

Session Management

Used in a conventional fashion, terminal emulation software can adequately manage sessions—albeit one session at a time. In the event that multiple sessions are needed, a new instance of the emulation software must be started to accommodate the need. Of course, this raises concerns of memory and other resource requirements such as network connections. Depending on the vendor, it may also result in licensing issues. The capability to open multiple sessions and manage them as one transaction is essential for the emulation software to be successful in the e-Business Integration domain.

The IBM 3270 and 5250 data streams are transported over different types of sessions or logical units (LU 7—display session, LU 4—printer session). The session management feature should be capable of managing different types of sessions and transporting the appropriate data streams as one transaction in the larger integration flow domain.

Exception Management

With all the aforementioned technical challenges and complexities, handling exceptions and taking corrective actions are critical features. The capability to define proper changes to a flow based on exceptions is essential for successful integration. Exceptions can arise because of physical connectivity problems, application-level problems, or even screen-scraping problems. Sometimes legacy application screens are changed, causing the screen-scraping functions to fail. Being able to isolate errors in the right areas helps resolve mainframe integration problems faster and better.

The diagram in Figure 14.5 captures the essential components of terminal emulation software and their relationships required for its successful use in the integration domain.

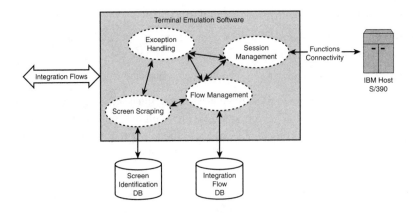

FIGURE 14.5

Essential components of terminal emulation software.

Modes of Terminal Emulation

Changing business processes in an e-Business environment results in changes to the legacy integration flows. Your ability to test changes before deploying them in a production environment is more critical in the mainframe application domain because most of these applications are mission critical. Corrupting the underlying databases with bad data is usually not acceptable in these environments. Hence, any terminal emulation software that will be used to enable legacy integration needs to support the following different modes of operation:

- User mode
- Design-time mode
- Test mode
- Runtime mode

User Mode

The user mode is the standard feature enabling end users to run a mainframe application on a desktop PC. The software can emulate both the 3270 and 5250 terminals. Although this mode doesn't have a big role in the integration perspective, having this feature will enable users to use the same software to run the applications directly.

Design-Time Mode

In design-time mode, the emulation software can connect to the actual mainframe application and execute it mainly to capture or record the screen flow and store it as a single flow. This flow could change in the future, requiring updates to the screen navigation or even including adding other flows. The benefit of executing mainframe applications in this mode is the ability to define required integration flows based on the application screens. Identifying the screens and storing them in a repository are also possible in this mode. Essentially, the design-time mode gives the users the ability to define the mainframe integration flows.

Test Mode

Testing integration flows using a test database is critical to the success of this technology. Simple errors in screen scraping result in runtime exceptions and deployment delays. Often the session management features and physical connectivity need to be tested as well. High-end terminal emulation software includes test mode features, but these features need to be extended for integration flow testing as well.

Runtime Mode

The runtime mode can fetch the correct integration flows from the database as well as the required screen definitions and identifications. This mode is different from the user mode in which end users access the host applications directly. The runtime mode is required for automation of the integration flows and transactions.

Without these different modes in the emulation software, deploying it in the integration domain is difficult. Users should recognize the difference between accessing mainframe applications using PCs and integrating mainframe applications using emulation techniques.

Summary

The mainframe technology domain is vast and far reaching. Undoubtedly, this chapter has only scratched the surface. It focused on the IBM mainframe and the most generalized integration methods, namely terminal emulation. The discussions uncovered how traditional terminal emulation software is not sufficiently comprehensive as an integration medium. Additional advanced features such as flow management, enhanced session management, a richer set of APIs, and the capability to support different modes (design-time, runtime, and test) are essential. With these features, terminal emulation can be very useful in enabling integration of mainframe applications for e-Business.

The advantage of using terminal emulation is its nonintrusive nature. Integration can also be achieved at the data level, but this approach doesn't enable the reuse of business logic embedded in the mainframe applications. Discussions on integrating IBM mainframe databases (DB2, IMS, VSAM, and so on) warrant separate chapters or even books, but suffice it to say that none provide the kind of seamless interaction provided by the terminal emulation approach. IBM is by no means standing still. It has recognized the need for its mainframe users to integrate with other e-Business applications and technologies. Eventually, newer tools based on IBM's e-Business technologies, such as WebSphere (IBM's application server) and MQSeries (IBM's messaging and queuing platform), will evolve and provide other viable options for integrating with legacy systems.

14

INTERFACING WITH
LEGACY
APPLICATIONS

e-Business Integration Practices

e-Business Integration Methodology: Steps to Success

"Time is a luxury you don't have."
—Ricardo Montalban as Khan in Star Trek II: The Wrath of Khan

IN THIS CHAPTER

The e-Business revolution has challenged conventional business thinking and practices and in the process has changed the business environment. The resulting new economy is based on a new set of rules for which the defining parameters of success are directly related to e-Business. Of course, the notion of being an e-Business is open to broad interpretation. Some corporations naively believe having Web "brochure-ware" and an email address is sufficient for the new economy. Of course, as many companies are beginning to understand, becoming an e-Business will incorporate not only reaching customers via the Web but also leveraging the Internet throughout the organization. Using the Internet means linking with partners and integrating processes and data. This means that succeeding with e-Business Integration initiatives becomes vitally important in this new economy.

The intent of this chapter is to provide you with a set of principles, guidelines, and a process for succeeding in an e-Business Integration project. This chapter will not cover specific practices; they are reserved for the following chapter. Instead, it will define an e-Business Integration methodology as a framework for thinking, planning, and implementing your e-Business Integration projects.

Why an e-Business Integration Methodology?

The question of why you would want to use an e-Business Integration methodology can be posed with two points in mind. First, why is a methodology important? Second, why do you need a methodology specifically for e-Business Integration? Wouldn't a general methodology applied to software development suffice?

Let me start by addressing the first question. A methodology is important for e-Business Integration for the same reason it's important for any other technical project. Methodologies are defined and adhered to for two primary reasons:

> To reduce risk and increase probability for success
>
> To achieve repeatability in your projects

No methodology in the world can guarantee success. However, a methodology should identify the processes and guidelines that will increase the probability that the project will succeed. Furthermore, it should ensure continued success in future projects.

Now that I've addressed the importance of a methodology, I'll focus on why a specific e-Business Integration methodology is important. The primary reason is that unique aspects of integration projects require a separate methodology and specific set of practices. Generic processes used for software development can be employed, but something gets lost in the translation to an e-Business Integration project. Inevitably, unique aspects of an e-Business

Integration project end up being shortchanged. Some of these unique characteristics are as follows:

- **Diverse skill requirements**—Integration projects require diverse skills spanning hardware-, software-, and application-specific knowledge. A typical corporate IT environment requires expertise on Windows, UNIX, and the mainframe.

- **Cross-organizational requirements**—Integration projects often touch various organizations in a corporation. This can lead to the need to skillfully traverse nontechnical issues such as project ownership and parochial attitudes regarding sharing information.

- **Technology requirements**—Integration projects require a high level of technical proficiency. They involve building infrastructure through applying off-the-shelf products in combination with custom-coded components. These projects are sensitive to requirements such as performance, scalability, and "mean time between failure."

- **Project cycle requirements**—Integration projects have their own cycle and rhythm of design, development, and deployment that are different from a typical application development project.

These characteristics necessitate a different approach to the projects that takes into account the unique attributes of e-Business Integration. In this chapter, I'll cover the "macro" methodology—the broad phases of an e-Business Integration project. At each of the phases, I will drill down to discuss the methodology, processes, and practices at the "micro" level.

Phases of the e-Business Integration Methodology

The e-Business Integration methodology set forth here is a series of steps beginning from setting the e-Business vision to evaluating the success of the integration projects. The methodology is composed of four basic phases, as shown in Figure 15.1.

1. **Strategy phase**—The first phase focuses on setting the business and technology goals. It is during this phase that business and technology objectives are aligned and a vision for the initiative is crafted.

2. **Planning phase**—This phase involves all planning, both technical and nontechnical in nature. This phase is essential to setting the project in motion and ensuring that the right foundation is in place for project execution. As an example, research is often conducted during this phase to determine technical feasibility.

3. **Implementation phase**—This phase entails the actual fulfillment of the strategic vision. Often, it is conducted in multiple implementation stages. This phase, which has other subphases and processes, is the primary focus of this chapter.

15

e-BUSINESS
INTEGRATION
METHODOLOGY

4. **Evaluation phase**—As you might conclude from the name, this phase is to evaluate the success of the implemented projects and plan for further expansion. Most organizations do not achieve all the goals and objectives in their first attempt. Practices in this phase ensure progression toward a self-learning and improving organization.

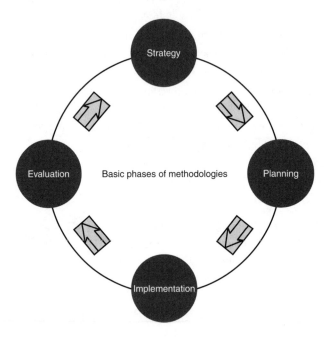

Figure 15.1
The four e-Business Integration methodology phases.

Strategy Phase

The first step can often be the most important. That could be said of the strategy phase. The primary objective of the strategy phase is to translate the corporate business objectives to a technology strategy. Business and technology intersect at this point. In a sense, the strategy for e-Business Integration is best crafted within the context of the broader corporate e-Business strategy. That is why the corporate e-Business vision must be well understood. The e-Business Integration strategy will emerge to serve the needs of the e-Business.

Formulating the e-Business Integration strategy requires applying the principles described in the following sections.

Principle 1: Know Yourself

Knowing yourself simply means understanding your corporate strategy for e-Business. As I said earlier, the e-Business Integration strategy is best crafted within the context of the broader corporate e-Business strategy. That is why knowing your company's e-Business vision is vital. The integration strategy will emerge to serve the broader corporate strategy.

Knowing yourself also means knowing your resources and capabilities. It means soberly assessing your strengths and weaknesses as an organization, both corporately and then specifically to the IT function (I am assuming that the IT organization is driving the e-Business Integration initiative). For instance, you may evaluate your IT function and realize that although the organization is technically strong, it is weak in project management. Hence, undertaking a complex, multiphase project may incur tremendous risk. Or your evaluation may turn up negative perceptions that other functional groups may have of the IT organization that will affect your ability to execute.

What should emerge out of an exercise of "knowing yourself" is a list of strengths and weaknesses of your IT organization as well as the broader corporation as it pertains to the integration initiative.

Principle 2: Know Your Customers

Just as knowing your business and processes is important, so is the need to know your customers. The term *customer* applies in the broadest sense. It refers to both internal customers as well as external customers. Internal customers refer to all the stakeholders of the e-Business Integration initiative. In an integration project in which you are linking your customer relationship management (CRM) system with your custom inventory system, the internal customers are the customer service organization and possibly sales management. External customers can be more than the traditional "end customers" in an e-Business model. Especially in a dynamic open B2B environment, external customers may be partners or suppliers. For instance, a supplier may have an interest in knowing when an inventory of parts reaches a low point so as to trigger an automatic new shipment of parts. Getting this information may require tying the inventory system to the supplier's warehouse shipping program.

Ultimately, knowing your customers means listing the stakeholders and their particular vested interest in your project. It also means understanding their high-level business and technical requirements that play into your integration initiative.

Principle 3: Understand the e-Business Models

Understanding the e-Business models means more than simply grappling with whether your implementation will service the B2C versus the B2B model. Certainly, you need to understand the broad e-Business vision, either in terms of how the integration project may enable a B2C site in generating business or fulfilling orders. But when I speak of understanding the e-Business models, I mean understanding the significance of integration in enabling the e-Business—in other words, understanding the *business* in e-Business. That's vital to bringing significance to your integration initiatives. It also helps in planning and applying initiatives in the long-term technology strategy. For instance, if your e-Business Integration initiative enables the HR department to allow employees to adjust their payroll deductions and 401K holdings online, it brings significance to your project. It also allows you to apply quantitative savings to a return on investment (ROI) calculation.

The other aspect of understanding the e-Business models pertains to looking at the integration patterns that might be applied in your e-Business initiative. The primary patterns covered in Chapter 3, "e-Business Integration Patterns," provide you with a basis for understanding what you are attempting to accomplish technically.

Principle 4: Communicate Your Strategy

The best vision or strategy remains unfulfilled when not communicated properly. An important practice is to document the strategy and communicate it to the stakeholders on a regular basis. A well-understood strategy enables all participants to work toward the common goal.

Based on the principles outlined previously, the strategy phase should yield the following results and deliverables:

Strategy statement—The strategy statement should capture the e-Business Integration vision and strategy. This statement should describe the integration strategy in terms of the broad e-Business objectives. It should be concise (anywhere from two paragraphs to two pages) but should briefly describe the business and technical goals of the project.

Stakeholder identification—The strategy phase should be used to formally identify the stakeholders. Once again, this includes both internal and external stakeholders. This information must include executives who have a vested interest. Depending on the scope of the project, they could be division presidents or even the CEO. For strategic projects, as the e-Business Integration initiatives often are, executive support is critical. Obtain that support up front. Functional groups affected by or benefiting from the projects are also internal stakeholders. External stakeholders may include strategic partners who are aware and affected by the project.

ROI in terms of ROM—The strategy phase should provide an ROI estimate in terms of rough order of magnitude (ROM) calculations. This estimate guides the level of investment and educates the stakeholders about the quantifiable benefit of the initiative.

e-Business Integration overview—The strategy should describe the scope of the "problem" and yield an overview of the technical solution. This is a general systems view of the proposed technical solution. It should identify systems affected, the e-Business models, and the general scope of the work to be done. It should describe the "macro architecture" of the solution, accompanied by figures and technical discussion.

Primary execution steps—Finally, the strategy phase should seek to address how the project will proceed. It should lay out general milestones and phases of progression as the project moves forward. It should also be explicit in seeking funding and approval if this is not assumed.

Planning Phase

Organizations that succeed understand this maxim: Strategy = Execution. A strategy without a corresponding execution plan is just wishful thinking. That is what makes the planning phase so important. During the planning phase, the execution plan is put in place. This phase includes the activities described in the following sections.

Research

Research is an important activity that is continuously conducted during the planning phase. It is conducted as a parallel activity, yielding information in support of generating deliverables in this phase, as shown in Figure 15.2.

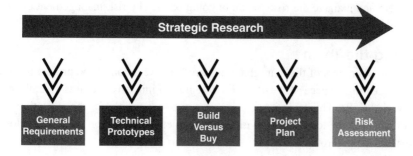

FIGURE 15.2
Strategic research with deliverables

Strategic Research

Strategic research starts with research of the problem space, identifying the potential risks and technical issues. It involves educating yourself about the technology products and technical hurdles to overcome. It should result in a list of technology vendors with viable technical solutions. As a result of conducting research during the strategy phase, the primary "build versus buy" decisions are made.

General Requirements

A primary activity of the planning phase is to gather business and technical requirements. At this point, they are not specifications of the solution, but general requirements of the project derived from the primary objective of the project, the proposed solution, and input from the stakeholders. A requirements document should be generated as part of the planning phase.

Project Task Plan

What should emerge through this planning phase are definitive high-level plans for execution. These plans should include a breakdown of the project into primary modules of development activity. Each module should identify primary tasks with interlinked dependencies. Of course, the use of a project planning tool such as MS Project is essential in crafting a project plan, but the most important tool is simply your own cognitive ability to systematically break down the broad project into more consumable pieces and then identify the tasks within each piece.

Resource Plan

The resource plan supports the project task plan. It actually starts by identifying special skills needed to execute the outlined tasks. As discussed earlier, integration projects are unique in the way they require such diverse skills. A resource plan identifies the necessary skills needed to execute the plan and the number of resources needed in different parts of the project.

Risk Management Document

What is derived from research and planning is a set of known risks. It is vitally important to document them and manage the risks on an ongoing basis. The risk management document is a living document that gets updated throughout the life of the project.

Assembling the Team

Finally, the core members of the team that will drive the execution of the project need to be assembled. Executing a successful e-Business Integration initiative requires assembling a core team with varied skills. This team is the primary group responsible for the execution of the project. Constructing the team begins with defining roles within the project. The following list defines some of the key roles in the project:

- **Executive sponsor**—Consider this person as the corporate "Integration Czar." This individual should represent executive sponsorship of the project. The executive sponsor should ensure that the corporation continues to support the project and is responsible for providing project visibility at the highest levels.

- **Project director**—This person is the operational manager for the project and is ultimately responsible for the success of the project. This person manages the schedule, budget, and resource planning. The project director reconciles competing objectives of schedule, function, and quality. It's not an easy job by any means, but it's well suited for someone who loves to be in the center of the action.

- **Chief architect**—This individual is responsible for crafting the technical solution and deriving the architecture. The chief architect is the senior technical leader on project team and can garner the respect of most if not all the technical members of the team. This person needs to be skilled at driving technical requirements and facilitating technical discussions.

- **Integration analyst**—This is a "specialized" role, not typical of most development projects. Just as a DBA specializes in designing and managing databases, an integration analyst is a specialized role around the needs of an integration project. This individual is responsible for logical modeling of the integration solution and the analysis of integration patterns. The integration analyst bridges the gap between the logical models and physical design of the system.

- **Business domain analyst**—This role is responsible for interacting with the individual business managers or stakeholders. The business analyst must understand the business needs and be able to communicate them to the rest of the team. Expect this person to work closely with the integration analyst.

- **Development team**—As with any development team, it should consist of the technical talent to design and deliver the solution. This team is responsible for designing, developing, testing, and deploying the technical solution. This team also performs technical research and due diligence on any technology applied in the project.

Implementation Phase

After completing the planning phase, you are now ready to implement. At this stage, plans turn into reality. The implementation phase is composed of these four separate stages of activity:

1. Initiating implementation
2. Designing implementation
3. Constructing implementation
4. Deploying implementation

Initiating Implementation

The initial stage of implementation should result in two objectives. The first is the generation of a detailed specification. This is accomplished by taking the general requirements gathered from the planning phase and defining the details behind those requirements. It also incorporates specific requirements pertaining to integration solutions. A sample of these special requirements include the following:

Performance—These are performance throughput requirements. They are sometimes measured in terms of messages transmitted between two points or transformation operations (for example, messages/sec, transformations/hour).

Availability—These requirements define metrics for measuring the availability of the integration services. Metrics may sometimes be expressed as mean time between failures or continuous uptime.

Scalability—This requirement is not about performance, although the two are related. Scalability defines how many systems can be supported without nonlinear degradation.

Platform support—Requirements for platform support are straightforward. They should specify the platform versions supported by the integration solution. For a Java-based integration solution, the version of the Java Virtual Machine should also be specified.

Application version support—Although not always apparent, the versions of the end applications should also be specified as part of the requirements.

During the initiation stage, conducting a proof of concept to validate the viability of any proposed solution is advisable. The proof of concept is used to evaluate and exercise the technology tools for use in the project. It should be a throwaway prototype that validates that the primary requirements can be accomplished. It assists the project leaders by doing the following:

- Provides a measure of understanding regarding the complexity of the project
- Confirms the primary tasks needed to be accomplished in the project
- Surfaces specific technical barriers and attempts to work through them
- Validates that the technology used will address requirements
- Develops a prototype of the macro architecture and validates that it has no fatal flaws

A word of caution: my experience is that it is easy to get carried away in this stage in an endless cycle of ongoing research that yields a new set of technical issues, which, in turn, need researching and prototyping. Focus only on technical issues that incorporate significant risk into the project. In short, keep this stage short.

After initiating implementation, you will have a detailed specification document in which you have selected primary tools for implementation and identified significant technical risks. Now you are ready to move on to design.

Designing Implementation

Designing implementation begins with modeling. Typically, you should focus on two kinds of modeling: business process modeling and data modeling.

Business process modeling, or logical modeling, refers to a set of techniques used to analyze and represent the business domain. The fundamental goal of business process modeling is to better understand the business domain from three perspectives:

Understanding the business function entities and how they inter-relate

Understanding the flow of business processes throughout the organization

Understanding the systems and data acted on or participating in the business process

The third point stresses the importance of understanding the relevant application data elements and how they relate to each other. It requires the development of an e-Business Integration Data Model (eDM). eDM is simply an extension of the enterprise data models engineered around enterprise data. However, it describes a subset of the enterprise data, encompassing only data relevant to the activity of integration. It also includes documents received and sent to B2B transaction participants as part of the data model.

The technique employed for generating an eDM is basic data modeling, involving the use of entity-relationship diagrams (ERD). You derive the eDM by building the ERD(s) for the logical data externalized by the integrated applications. The resulting artifact allows you to assure a normalized flow of data as you design your integration solution.

Finally, designing the implementation means crafting an architecture for the integration solution. Typically, I have found it valuable to analyze and represent this architecture in three primary views:

- Collaboration view
- Layered view
- Physical deployment view

Collaboration View

The collaboration view is a standard design presentation expressed in the Unified Modeling Language (UML). In UML, the collaboration view is a type of object interaction diagram. It represents the static and dynamic relationships between objects within a system. It permits the modeling of coupling between objects as well as message-based interaction. This flexibility makes it ideal for capturing various integration patterns, even message-based systems found in EAI architectures. Figure 15.3 presents an example of a collaboration architecture view.

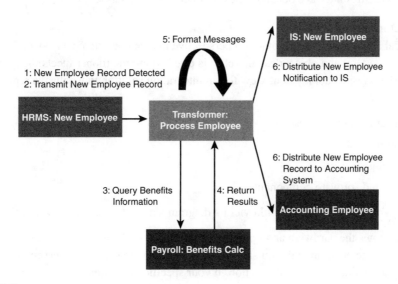

FIGURE 15.3
Collaboration Architecture View.

Ultimately, in developing the collaboration view, you are seeking to actually derive the primary components of the architecture. As noted in the Unified Software Development Process (Unified Modeling Language User Guide, [Booch, Jacobsen, Rumbaugh]), three kinds of objects can be identified during this activity: control objects, entity objects, and boundary objects. Control objects, as denoted by the name, exercise control and coordination of other objects. This includes transaction management and other activities common to integration architectures. Entity objects directly model business domain entities or persistent information. As such, these objects are not typically subject to dynamic interaction. Boundary objects, on the other hand, capture dynamic interactions with external entities such as a user or an application.

Layer View

The layer view often depicts architecture in terms of a layered "stack." You can derive the layer architecture view by mapping the hierarchical segments of the architecture. You begin the lowest layer as representing the base primitive functions and subsequent layers with increasing functional complexity.

Besides creating another pretty picture, what do you gain by representing the architecture in a layer view? First, this view is an organizational tool. It helps identify objects and services that share the same level of functional complexity or tasks. Using it is often the easiest way to express a complex architecture. As I've often said, it's so elegantly simple that even the marketing guys will understand it. Second, it creates abstraction and segmentation between the different services such that the constructed architecture will actually be more extensible. The layer view identifies interface dependencies between different service APIs.

Physical Deployment View

The physical deployment view provides a perspective that can be often overlooked in the midst of modeling, pattern, and object design. Yet, it is often where the rubber meets the road, at least on paper. The physical deployment view for an integration solution must always represent the following:

- Application and data resources
- Hardware systems
- Operating systems
- Distributed software components

Accounting for the these items should yield a diagram similar to the one shown in Figure 15.4.

This figure shows the hardware and operating system deployed and explicitly identifies the applications in the environment. You should use this method to capture the essential information of how a running system will function in your specific environment.

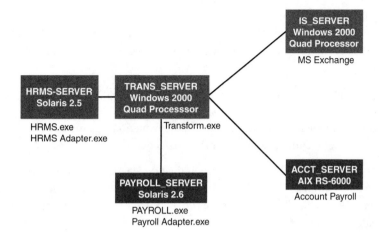

FIGURE 15.4

Physical deployment view.

The three views offered here are geared for a project that is not primarily a custom-coding solution, but one in which custom development supplements vendor tools. That does not preclude the value of using other object diagrams, such as package diagrams, to represent the class-level design.

Finally, before I leave this topic, I would like to offer this piece of advice. Although I have found that each view leads me down a useful analysis path in creating a sound architecture, sometimes applying all three views is unnecessary. Apply your own judgment and feel no obligation to develop all three views, especially in trivially simple scenarios. Travel light; use only what is necessary for your integration scenario.

Constructing the Implementation

At this stage, the development of the designed solution takes place. This process involves creating a detailed design, writing code, testing, and integrating third-party vendor technologies. In most ways, code development in an integration project doesn't vary a great deal from any software project. The methodology applied in this phase should be typical of any software development project.

However, in addition to a typical software development methodology such as Rational's Unified Process, there are "best practices" that pertain to developing and testing an integration project. I plan to cover these practices in the next chapter. Because they are not formal methods but rather a set of practical tips and practices applied with discretion to an integration development project, I chose not to address them in this chapter.

Deploying the Implementation

After the solution is crafted, it must still be deployed for production use. Deployment is about the delivery of the solution to the user community. It also includes the subsequent management of that solution.

This stage may be the most neglected in the implementation project cycle. It may lack the high-charged energy of the inception phase, creativity of design, and satisfaction of constructing your solution, but, nonetheless, this stage of implementation ensures the delivery and use of the solution. It directly correlates to customer satisfaction.

The two primary aspects to deployment are preproduction staging and management. Preproduction staging validates the solution in an operational "sandbox." The preproduction systems environment should closely mirror the production infrastructure as much as possible. Often it is a scaled-down version of the production systems, with similar platforms and operating systems represented. In many applications, preproduction is an opportunity to train the users on the system, but because integration projects are usually not mostly about end users, but rather integrated data resources, that objective is somewhat obscured. For an integration solution, the preproduction staging still serves a number of purposes:

- It performs a final systems acceptance test to validate conformance to requirements.
- It provides the opportunity to simulate real-life production scenarios.
- It provides a graceful bridge to production systems.

Before the preproduction is completed and the system is moved online to the production environment, you need to put together a production checklist and verify it for check-off.

The second aspect of deployment is management of the deployed system. Management includes a number of activities, including the following:

Installation—Installation encompasses both first-time installations as well as upgrades to existing systems. The deployment stage must provide guidelines and procedures for installation and upgrades.

Version management—Each version of the integration solution components must be managed. In an architecture that is made up of several different vendor products and custom-coded components, version management ensures that the baseline of a working system is always maintained and dependencies between entities are known. Upgrades are conducted with order, taking into account dependencies.

Runtime management—An integration solution should be constructed and deployed with manageability in mind. The different aspects of runtime systems management include managing availability, performance, response time, notification, exception handling, and control. The goal of manageability for your runtime integration system should be a "single point of control"—that is, the ability to manage your entire environment from a single console. This console should also be integrated with a standard systems management framework, such as IBM Tivoli, CA Unicenter, or HP OpenView.

Evaluation Stage

Evaluation or assessment of your project is a healthy and necessary phase in completing the e-Business Integration initiative. The evaluation phase is not mere formality but is critical to an effective and successful e-Business organization. The purpose for the evaluation phase is four-fold:

- To reinforce the best practices
- To uncover new effective practices
- To eliminate outmoded or ineffective practices
- To measure and develop metrics

You need to reinforce existing best practices through every cycle. Organizations and project teams need to be reminded of what works and, more importantly, "why we do what we do." During the course of projects, new practices developed in the heat of battle add value and refine the process. They need to be surfaced and incorporated into the methodology. Similarly, practices that were once applicable may be deemed ineffective or outmoded. They simply need to be replaced.

Finally, the last objective is to develop metrics for measurement. However, it raises the question of what is to be evaluated in this phase. Should you seek to measure the project, methodology, people, or solution? The answer really depends on your organization. I believe the ultimate measurement is effectiveness. Is your e-Business Integration initiative effective? Effectiveness can be measured by different business parameters such as customer satisfaction, ROI, or efficiency gains in business process. You could also measure in terms of technical indicators such as completion of project within defined scope, rate of user adoption, system performance, or availability. The point is that you need to determine key indicators that define what it means for the e-Business initiative to be successful and measure them with each cycle.

Summary

Succeeding with an e-Business Integration initiative takes more than simply understanding technology or business models. Many organizations are unable to succeed for lack of consistent execution. Consistent execution can be accomplished only through a proven methodology.

15

E-BUSINESS INTEGRATION METHODOLOGY

This chapter introduced the following four phases of an e-Business Integration methodology designed to ensure successful execution:

1. Strategy
2. Planning
3. Implementation
4. Evaluation

This four-phased methodology provides a cyclical set of steps that are effective, consistent, and repeatable for a successful project outcome. Each successive step builds on the preceding step as the project moves from phase to phase.

The strategy phase ensures that business objectives are defined and translated into an actionable technical strategy. During the planning phase, research is conducted, general requirements are gathered, and plans are defined. The implementation phase involves execution of the plans defined in the preceding phase, which means initiating, designing, constructing, and deploying the implemented solution. Finally, each cycle of e-Business Integration projects must include an evaluation phase such that a "feedback loop" is introduced into the process.

As Figure 15.5 shows, each phase begins with key inputs that yield specific deliverables. These inputs are often best practices but can also be other external sources of information or influence. Each phase is designed to result in an outcome and will generate a collection of artifacts that provide a track for successful execution.

For instance, the planning phase incorporates requirements gathering, risk assessment, task and resource planning, and technical research. Other inputs into this phase may be industry standards such XML or J2EE. The resulting outputs from this phase include a project plan and risk management document.

The next chapter fills in the gaps in the methodology by providing a set of practical tips and practices for implementation. It will touch on aspects of design, development, testing, and deployment of the integration solution. These practical tips, though not defined as part of a methodology, can still make the difference between success and failure.

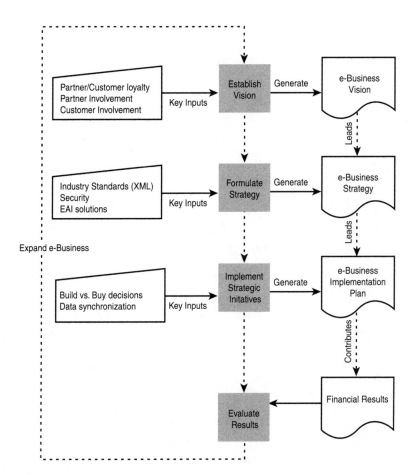

FIGURE 15.5

e-Business Integration phase inputs and resulting artifacts.

Practical Steps for a Successful Integration Project

16

"The race is not to the swift or the battle to the strong, nor does food come to the wise or wealth to the brilliant or favor to the learned; but time and chance happen to them all."
—Ecclesiastes 9:11

IN THIS CHAPTER

In the preceding chapter, I discussed a life-cycle methodology for e-Business Integration projects. It takes you through the crafting of the strategy, planning, implementation, and finally deployment. Such a methodology offers a repeatable process for successful execution. However, it doesn't cover a myriad of best practices and practical tips that may be used in the course of execution. The purpose of this chapter is to fill in the "white space" in the methodology with best practices that speak specifically to the task of implementing an integration project. Implementing these practical tips can often mean the difference between a solution that works and one that's planned to work.

Borrowing a page from the popular personal productivity guru, Stephen Covey, I have identified my own seven habits or practices of a highly successful e-Business Integration solution:

1. Cultivating an understanding of priorities

2. Constructing in layers

3. Profiling performance early and often

4. Building in resiliency

5. Embracing comprehensive testing

6. Addressing secondary scenarios

7. Building with deployment in mind

As I discuss the significance and details of each practice in the rest of this chapter, you will find that some warrant multiple pages of discussion, whereas others are relatively brief. Regardless of the length of discussion, I believe that each of these habits can be absolutely life-saving for your projects.

Cultivating an Understanding of Priorities

I would understand if this first practice of cultivating an understanding of priorities sounds a little too philosophical or "touchy-feely" for you. It's really not meant to be. The point behind this seemingly philosophical maxim is to get you to focus on the important technical details in your solution; it's about cultivating an understanding of the technical priorities. The technical priorities of your e-Business Integration solution are represented in a hierarchical order in Figure 16.1, beginning with runtime reliability.

These priorities are not absolute, but they are generally true of most integration deployments. An understanding of these priorities should drive every stage of the development of the e-Business Integration solution from requirements gathering to deployment. During each staged activity, an inappropriate focus of technical priorities can be misleading and time-consuming.

Runtime reliability is most important because e-Business Integration is about the runtime exchange of information between applications. When it is implemented, it becomes part of the enterprise infrastructure. This implies that it is business-critical and costly to displace. It becomes as vital to conducting business operations as the applications it integrates. If the integration infrastructure isn't reliable, nothing else matters—not how the system performs or how easily you can design a solution.

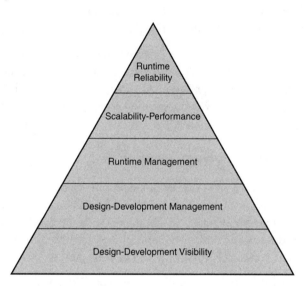

FIGURE 16.1

Hierarchical order of technical priorities.

As I've stated in previous chapters, scalability and performance are separate but related topics. However, for the purpose of this discussion, I address them as a singular priority for the sake of simplicity. Runtime scalability and performance are typically the next in importance after runtime reliability because most organizations have a specific requirement for the latency of data within the enterprise. In the exchange of information or execution of an automated process, there is often a required level of performance or the need to be able to integrate a number of additional applications. These requirements are important to identify early in the requirement development stage because they can govern the design and construction parameters of an integration system.

The manageability of the running system is also a priority that can get overlooked. The systems management aspect of deploying an integration solution includes installing and upgrading mechanisms and managing availability and performance of the runtime infrastructure. The integration solution should be manageable from a single point of control and interoperate with other third-party enterprise systems management tools, such as IBM Tivoli or CA Unicenter.

Lower in the priority scale are design-time aspects such as design-time manageability and usability. Design-time manageability pertains to how the data models and source code are maintained. The fact that these aspects reside lower in the priority scale doesn't mean that they're not important. In fact, the management of technical documentation, data models, and source code is vital to ongoing maintenance. As these are important aspects of any development project, there are many available tools on the market to address this need.

These priorities may seem obvious, but often projects fail because of a lack of understanding for what is of primary importance. I don't mean that design-time usability doesn't matter, only that it should fall beneath runtime reliability in the order of importance. This order of importance should be reflected in the relative time spent on each priority in requirements, design, construction, and deployment.

Constructing in Layers

The notion of iterative development is now common wisdom in the software development community. Instead of a traditional process of requirement specifications, architecture, design, coding, and testing, most practitioners of object-oriented software development practices advocate a phased iterative development cycle. With integration projects, it is important to couple this iterative cycle with an approach of constructing in segments.

In some ways, e-Business Integration is really not very complicated. The problem of e-Business Integration can fundamentally be broken down into these four basic layered segments, as shown in Figure 16.2:

1. Process flow
2. Application access
3. Transformation
4. Transport

You can attack the construction of the solution by breaking the task into these four layered segments. After the macro-level view of the entire architecture is developed, each segment should be designed, engineered, and tested as independent components within the system. This systematic approach offers the following benefits. First, it allows you to validate each functional segment of your solution before constructing the whole solution. Second, it leads to better construction and debugging of the integration system. Finally, it permits some degree of concurrent parallel development to take place.

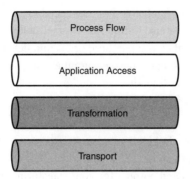

FIGURE 16.2

Integration Solution Layers.

Process Flow

Modeling the business process flow is not an essential step to your constructing the integration system. Modeling, from a business process view, is useful and preferable in a large corporate integration project, but in many simple integration scenarios, it may simply be overkill. For instance, if you plan to integrate three systems together in a relatively limited scale, there may be little in the way of business processes to be defined. In these instances, it may be easier to take a data integration view and begin with simply a model of data flow between the applications concerned.

In a larger-scale project, beginning by modeling the business process is generally preferable for two reasons. First, this approach more accurately models the real world of business activity. Instead of dealing with the movement of data, it deals with the process of business operations. Second, it allows participation and validation from the business users and stakeholders in a language they understand.

Constructing the business process flow involves an iterative cycle of modeling the business process, reviewing the process, validating the process through a series of practical use cases, and mapping the process activities to data resources. Often a prototype is not needed because business process integration is conducted at a logical level, and deeper analysis of data integration will be conducted later.

Application Access

Treating the entire integration problem space as discrete segments is valuable, never more so than when you are dealing with application access. As you learned in Chapter 9, "Using Adapters for Application Data Access," on adapters, application access is a critical part of integration.

Constructing the application access component may mean purchasing an adapter from a vendor or developing your own custom adapter code. In any case, this process begins with a normalized model of your enterprise data, as you learned in the preceding chapter. If you construct your own application adapter, you must also familiarize yourself with the available application access mechanisms. Regardless of whether you purchase or custom develop your adapter, this process also implies testing the adapter component to ensure that data is updated to and retrieved from the application consistently and accurately.

Transformation

As with application access, you should develop and test your transformation code as a separate entity. The transformation layer can be developed in parallel with the other layers with limited impact. For instance, the inputs and outputs for your transformation logic are the application messages that are derived from the application access segment. You can develop and test this transformation logic independent of the work done in developing application access components. Test drivers with mock data can be used to validate the transformation logic without linking to the actual applications.

Transport

Finally, the transport should be developed, tested, and tuned separately. When referring to the *transport*, I simply mean the communication mechanism used to transmit data between applications. It may be a synchronous mechanism such as Remote Method Invocation (RMI) or an asynchronous messaging medium such as Java Messaging Service (JMS). Validate your transport mechanism on points such as support for deployment platforms, performance requirements, handling for failure, and size of messages.

Profiling Performance Early and Often

One of the primary measured requirements of an integration system is performance. Very often, if a system fails to meet performance requirements, it is simply unusable. For that reason, performance profiling as practice should be conducted on a regular basis *during* the development cycle, not simply at the end. Doing so provides two primary benefits:

1. Getting a handle on performance throughput, system bottlenecks, and design limitations early in the development cycle is less costly. When you wait to the end to measure performance, detecting the problem areas becomes more difficult. You may also discover a fundamental design flaw that could have been far easier to correct during the development cycle.

2. Detecting performance limitations for a complete integration system can be difficult at the end because you are limited by what can be observed through monitoring the overall architecture. Optimizing at this point requires taking into account a host of variables, including network traffic, messaging throughput, and data conversion rates. Instead, each primary component could be profiled and optimized independently before being integrated with the rest of the architecture. Knowing the processing rates for each independent

unit allows you to predict the optimal processing rate of the overall system and proactively detect problem areas.

Conducting a Performance Profile

Performance profiling is not a single occurrence in the development life cycle but rather a cyclical process. The cycle of performance profiling can actually be broken down into four parts:

- Setting a technical baseline
- Monitoring
- Analysis
- Optimization

Performance profiling begins by setting a technical baseline. This means first determining the parameters for measurement. It involves asking yourself "What do I measure to determine the system performance?" It also involves determining which components should be monitored. Finally, it defines the kinds of tests to run for the purposes of validating the system.

After you have established the technical baseline, you can begin monitoring the system. This is the data collection portion of the performance profiling cycle and is commonly referred to as *benchmarking*. The monitoring mechanism in place may be inadequate and may require actual code instrumentation to be able to gather the necessary data.

In the analysis portion, you turn the raw performance data into statistics and information about the system performance. You may correlate system performance statistics with systems resource indicators, such as CPU utilization, memory utilization, or network traffic. Also in this portion, the hard work of determining boundary conditions of your system occurs. You may discover the performance of the system is not bound by code execution or CPU cycles but rather by the throughput of the wide area network.

The analysis phase, in turn, leads to an optimization phase in which corrective measures are enacted to improve performance. These measures may mean improving the hardware, correcting flaws in the software design, or simply tuning system parameters to get more processing throughput.

The Cyclical Nature of Performance Profiling

As mentioned previously, performance profiling is cyclical in nature and should be regarded as an iterative process. Also, the performance profiling cycle should be conducted at a component level before conducting it with the entire integration system. For example, if you have a basic integration system involving two applications, you can begin by profiling the data access components for each of the applications, the transformation engine, and the messaging service used for the system, as shown in Figure 16.3.

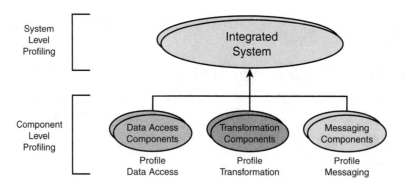

FIGURE 16.3

Steps for Profiling Integration System.

As you can see in Figure 16.3, after each component has been benchmarked and optimized, the system is built together in phases. Each phase of the overall system is optimized before moving on to the subsequent phase. During each cycle, you can learn more about the behavior and performance of the system.

Building in Resiliency

Resiliency describes the capability of a system to provide high availability for its services despite faults and exceptions. You could think of it as a measure of how fault tolerant the system is, although I prefer not to use the phrase *fault tolerance* because it implies clustering and other related technologies.

A concept you need to understand when delving into the arena of highly available and tolerant systems is something known as *mean time between failures* (MTBF), which is a measure of system uptime. MTBF measures the system uptime by referring to the length of time the system runs between its last and next failed condition. It is the mean of the running periods between these failed conditions and is measured on a percentage scale. An MBTF of 99.9 means that the system is down 0.1% of the time, which translates to approximately 8 hours and 45 minutes in a year.

Resiliency or fault tolerance—regardless of what you call it—is fundamentally an architecture issue. The concept of building resiliency needs to be adopted as a primary principle during the development process, beginning in the requirements and design phases. When resiliency is not addressed early in design, retrofitting it into the system can be costly. Here are a few ways you can construct a resilient and highly fault tolerant system:

1. Eliminate single points of failure.

2. Isolate effects of failure.

3. Minimize moving parts.

4. Implement failover mechanisms.

Eliminating Single Points of Failure

A single point of failure (SPOF) is the weakest link in your system architecture. Any failed component that causes your entire integration system to fail and experience down time is regarded as an SPOF. During the design of the system, time should be invested in reviewing the physical deployment architecture as well as software architecture looking for SPOF. This analysis should be conducted from the top down (analysis of a component view) as well as from the bottom up (analysis of a use case). After this analysis is complete, you may choose from several corrective measures to eliminate the SPOF. Corrective measures could range from the redesign of a software component, the application of redundant services, or the addition of fault management hardware configurations.

Isolating Effects of Failure

If a component failure occurs (and it eventually will, even in the most reliable systems), you need to limit the effect of the failure from cascading to other parts of the system. Some of the failure containment is a matter of the designed procedure. For example, if an adapter is receiving an application message and writing it to a message queue, you want to ensure that the adapter holds a copy of the message only *after* the messaging system has acknowledged that it has successfully delivered the message to its destination queue. This scenario is shown in Figure 16.4.

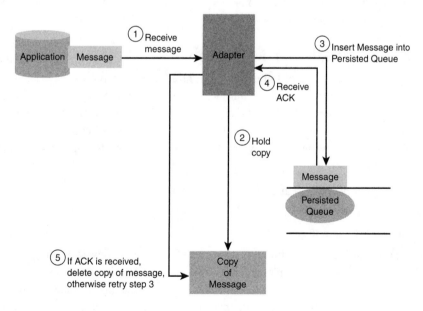

FIGURE 16.4
Designed for Ensuring Message Delivery.

If, for instance, the messaging system receives the message but crashes immediately before delivering it to the destination, the acknowledgment would not be returned, and the adapter would still have a copy of the application message to resubmit later.

Minimizing Moving Parts

Another principle to adhere to is reducing the number of distributed entities that require dependent links. In other words, consolidate your deployed servers. Distributed computing has encouraged the emergence of systems that do not require components to be co-located on the same physical machine. You could build an n-tier solution that has numerous primary components distributed on multiple machines and communicating either through a CORBA or distributed messaging infrastructure. But this doesn't mean that doing so always make sense. The more distributed your deployment becomes, the more dependent linkages it requires to function flawlessly. Thus, your deployment needlessly increases the opportunities for some aspect of the system to malfunction, and it also places a greater burden on managing each discretely deployed component. Figure 16.5 shows how a system with five primary components deployed separately has significantly more points of failure interjected than if these five components were deployed on two machines.

Furthermore, not only must these components be maintained, but in a peer-to-peer mode, the linkages between the components have to be maintained as well. If one segment of the network that jeopardizes a linkage goes down, the runtime system is compromised.

Implementing Failover Mechanisms

Even when you limit the effects of failure and minimize "moving parts" of the system, you still need to protect your points of potential failure within the system, especially for the SPOF. A system designed for resiliency implements failover mechanisms for critical system components. Certainly, a complete description of failure management options could warrant a separate book altogether, but I want to draw your attention to three ways to implement failover within your system architecture:

- Data management for high availability
- Software component clustering
- Hardware fault tolerant systems

One area of profound weakness within a system is the failure of the physical storage system such as disks. Resilient systems implement advanced data management facilities such as Redundant Array of Inexpensive Disks (RAID) or the rapidly emerging storage area networks (SAN). The idea behind RAID is to provide mechanisms for an array of disks to be organized and managed such that the disks and subsequently the critical data are redundant. Five levels of RAID lead to increasing levels of availability, beginning with RAID 1 and extending to RAID 5. (As a side note, RAID 0 does not provide redundancy.)

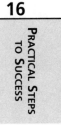

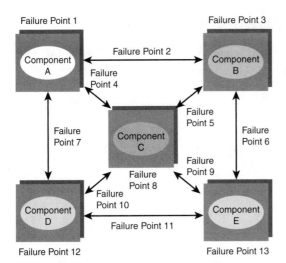

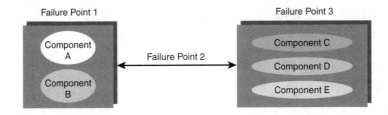

FIGURE 16.5
Points of failure exponentially grow as more machines are deployed.

SANs create a pool or network of storage devices that have the effect of decentralizing storage. When used in combination with RAID, a SAN can provide a high-performance, highly available storage mechanism.

Software component clustering refers to providing failover of critical software components through a software clustering solution. For example, using an application server such as WebLogic to host software components such as Enterprise Java Beans (EJB) provides software clustering. If an EJB fails before fulfilling a request, the clustering mechanism transparently activates another instance of that EJB to fulfill the request.

Finally, you can sometimes be so focused on designing the software architecture for redundancy and high availability that you fail to recognize that a hardware solution may be in order. Often the use of hardware failover or load-balancing systems may provide you with a level of reliability and service that is unattainable through software. Besides using RAID hardware, I recommend you explore the use of a relatively low-cost, load management/high availability hardware solution from RADware.

Embracing Comprehensive Testing

Tests of an integration solution should be comprehensive in nature and occur at multiple levels. These six kinds of basic tests should be run on the integration infrastructure:

- Component testing
- System testing
- Endurance testing
- Platform testing
- Performance-scalability testing
- Secondary scenario testing

Component Testing

As you learned earlier in this chapter, it is highly recommended that the primary functional components of the system be designed, developed, tested, and profiled individually before you conduct a comprehensive system test. This means preparing for component testing during the development cycle by developing test drivers, instrumentation "hooks" for measuring performance, and building test beds to simulate "live" data.

System Testing

After testing has been conducted at the component level, the integration system should be tested for functional compliance. This means executing on test plans that exercise both the design-time usage and runtime execution. Design-time testing involves testing the use of the configuration, data mapping, and transformation definition facilities. Runtime testing executes on specific data integration scenarios with a prepared test bed of data.

Endurance Testing

Endurance testing speaks to the need for runtime availability of the system. These long-running tests are particularly useful for ferreting out memory leaks that can appear randomly. The purpose is to validate the resiliency of the system over a defined period of time. For instance, in some systems that I've worked on, a system was required to run continuously for at least two weeks, or 336 hours, before the release is qualified for general availability. Of course, the idea is that the system should run for far more than two weeks, but the two weeks provided an opportunity to shake out the memory leaks and other more spurious problems.

Platform Testing

Enterprise integration often requires platform testing because most enterprise environments are not generally homogenous. The primary development and functional testing work usually occur on one or perhaps two platform types. They are referred to as the *reference platforms*. Platform testing needs to occur for additional platforms that need to be supported. Platform testing may not be as rigorous as the system tests on the reference platform, and the tests often conducted on these secondary platforms are regression tests. They are a subset of the full test suite conducted to generally validate the release.

Performance-Scalability Testing

I've already covered the importance of treating performance and scalability testing as part of the performance profiling activity. I've also discussed how performance profiling adds value to the development of your system. Additionally, load testing should be conducted to determine the boundary conditions of the system. This should be applied both in terms of a constant stream as well as in a burst mode.

With a constant stream of load, load is applied on a regular interval for an extended period of time. Applying a load of 50 messages per second for several hours may be an example. The constant stream of messages stresses the system message queues. Over a period of time, if the queues cannot be cleared properly, the result could be a backlog of messages and an overflow of your message queue.

Performance and scalability should also be determined by engaging in burst mode testing. Instead of applying a constant stream of data, this method of testing is conducted with the intent to overwhelm the system. For instance, instead of applying 50 messages per second for several hours, you may send a burst of 5,000 messages every minute for one hour and gauge whether the system is able to cope accordingly.

Secondary Scenario Testing

Secondary scenarios are covered in more detail in this next practice. For now, suffice it to say that testing needs to encompass not only how the system should function when presented with primary conditions for successful execution, but also what happens when secondary situations resulting from unpredictable failures or erroneous data occur. This type of testing should also be an essential element of any comprehensive test plan.

Addressing Secondary Scenarios

What are secondary scenarios? Here's an example: I experienced a secondary scenario just a few days ago when I logged on with my online broker planning to make a trade. Although no restrictions were in place, the system erroneously prevented me from selling shares in my portfolio. After hours of discussion with customer service, I eventually resorted to placing the trade through the phone instead. In other words, secondary scenarios are simply what occur when the system doesn't work as planned.

For integration systems, secondary scenarios emerge when the integration data flow isn't completed in the expected course of execution. Secondary scenarios need to be considered and accounted for throughout the design, development, and testing of the integration system. For instance, if an application rejects a message submitted for update, how does the integration system handle the rejected message? The system may retry for some specified number of times before logging the message to a failed message queue. No matter how rigorous a system is tested, unpredictable behavior and failures are inevitable. They may be caused by flawed code or hardware failures, or the course of execution may simply exceed the normal boundaries of the system.

Another example of a secondary scenario is shown in Figure 16.6. Here, the integration system is responsible for capturing data from a Web-based application for customers who want to receive a printed catalog. It cross-references a database of these customers to retrieve the mailing addresses, combines it with other data, and sends them to the subsidiary responsible for catalog sales.

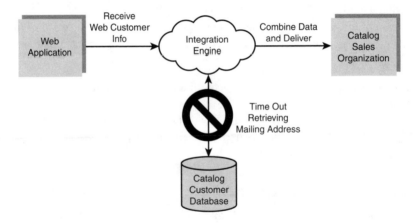

FIGURE 16.6
Example of Secondary Scenario.

You know how this system should work, but what occurs when the database server is too busy to service the request for mailing addresses and times out after a specified length of time? What does the system do to accommodate this unpredictable scenario, and how does it resolve the incomplete integration flow? Building systems that address secondary scenarios requires that you adhere to the following principles of system behavior:

- **Preservation of message**—In the event of a failed operation, the system should never result in the loss of messages or data packets.

- **Preservation of data integrity**—In the event of a failed operation, the system should preserve the integrity of messages. This means that the structure and content of the data should not be changed or compromised in any way.

- **Predefined exception handling**—Failed operations should have a predefined course of execution. If a given operation fails, the system should provide specific handling for the exception. This may mean retrying until successful or logging the failed message in an error file.

- **Graceful exits**—Operations that fail because of unavailable resources or critical errors should exit gracefully, returning the system to a consistent and known state. These operations should not cause an aborted end to the execution, leaving the integration data flow in an undetermined state. An undetermined state occurs when the state of the data is not reliable and a corrective course of action on the data is unknown.

Be faithful about addressing secondary scenarios during the design phase by examining each component and considering the effect of failure of a primary operation, such as updating an application. You should also consider what happens when the system is unable to account for operational dependencies being fulfilled. For instance, if a transformation operation requiring a combination of message A and message B fails because message B never arrives, an operational dependency has not been fulfilled. Also, consider the cascading effect of the failure of the operation. Does the failure to perform the transformation result in a halted business process? If so, the state of the remaining messages should be preserved such that they can be resubmitted for processing, albeit possibly triggered manually.

Building with Deployment in Mind

In my opinion, most project teams don't consider building with deployment in mind during the development phase. Of course, building this way is given passing consideration during the requirements and planning stages, but often in design and construction, it falls by the wayside. Yet, failure to consider this leads to ineffective and flawed systems. In some organizations, this failure is a result of IT organizational structure. A development team constructs the integration system while a separate systems management team deploys the solution.

Perhaps, instead of general good intentions, what is needed is to "spell out" specific ways teams can build with deployment in mind. I've tried to list a few here to keep all of us honest:

1. Build a traceable system.
2. Instrument components for monitoring.
3. Link to systems management frameworks.
4. Establish service-level agreements and test for compliance.
5. Build a deployment and management plan early.

Building a Traceable System

Trying to detect problems in distributed integration architectures can be very tricky. It can be particularly frustrating when the system provides little in the way of tracing the execution path.

Building traceability into the system allows you to debug the system during the development process as well as manage the system through a successful deployment. When a system is deployed in production, it introduces a new set of variables that simply cannot be duplicated in quality assurance environments. The introduction of "live" data and production applications with a full production user load may extend the parameters beyond what was tested in the engineering lab. Because traceability can affect performance of the system, turning it on with different trace levels should be an option.

Instrumenting System Components for Monitoring

The primary system components should be instrumented for monitoring. Key metrics about the availability, performance, and resource utilization should be collected on each of the components. This allows the system administrator to detect problem areas with system performance and correlate that information with the availability of sufficient system resources. This data can also be used in planning for increasing throughput capacity.

Linking to Systems Management Frameworks

Often systems management is considered at the end of the development cycle, often only when deployment planning begins. Interoperability with systems management frameworks such as IBM Tivoli or CA Unicenter should be considered early in the requirements stage and accounted for in design. This often means doing the following:

- Instrumenting the integration system to support SNMP. This step equates to firing SNMP traps based on system events and controlling system components via SNMP.

- Linking administration facilities of the integration system to the systems management framework. This allows the systems management framework to launch the administration console of the integration system.

Establishing Service-Level Agreements and Testing for Compliance

Service-level agreements (SLAs) are formal agreements regarding some aspect of the running system. That aspect is often linked to the performance and availability of the system. SLAs are an essential tool for managing and guiding your development parameters. They should be established as part of the requirements phase and tested for compliance during development and quality assurance.

Building a Deployment and Management Plan Early

Along the lines of considering the ongoing management of the deployed system not as a development afterthought but as a planned ingredient to the development process, I recommend that a deployment and management plan be constructed in the requirements phase. Just like the SLA, some of these requirements may find their way into the requirements document, but constructing this plan also means taking care of business on other fronts:

- Planning separate environments for development, testing, staging, pre-production, and production
- Detailing the installation mechanism used or defining how one should operate
- Defining the phases of deployment and then rolling out the schedule for each phase (that is, alpha, beta, pre-production, and production)
- Defining acceptance tests for each stage of deployment
- Planning a backup procedure that will be enacted for each stage
- Planning a disaster recovery mechanism for the deployed system. It could entail using a company that provides a service to store the code, configuration, and data offsite.

You can probably think of a few others, but the point is that great integration solutions are deployed on paper before they are deployed onsite.

Summary

This chapter covered more than simply theoretical methodologies. It provided practical insights on how to construct a solution based on proven practices. The seven key practices I covered begin with the importance of cultivating a priority framework and a methodical construction of the system. It also addresses the essential practices for profiling performance, building resiliency, testing, analyzing secondary scenario and deploying the system.

Building integration solutions that are extensible, high performing, and resilient is a difficult task. Although these practices are not deterministic—that is, they do not *guarantee* success—applying them reduces technical risks and establishes a foundation for successful implementation.

INDEX

S